SELLING TO
ZEBRAS

HOW *to* CLOSE 90% *of the* BUSINESS YOU PURSUE FASTER, MORE EASILY, *and* MORE PROFITABLY

JEFF KOSER & CHAD KOSER

GREENLEAF
BOOK GROUP PRESS

Published by Greenleaf Book Group Press
4425 S. Mo Pac Expy., Suite 600
Austin, TX 78735
www.greenleafbookgroup.com

Distributed by Greenleaf Book Group LLC

For ordering information or special discounts for bulk purchases, please contact Greenleaf Book Group LLC at 4425 S. Mo Pac Expy., Suite 600, Austin, TX 78735, (512) 891-6100.

Design and composition by Greenleaf Book Group LLC
Cover design by Greenleaf Book Group LLC

Microsoft product screen shots reprinted with permission from Microsoft Corporation.

Publisher's Cataloging-In-Publication Data
(Prepared by The Donohue Group, Inc.)

Koser, Jeff.
    Selling to zebras : how to close 90% of the business you pursue faster, more easily, and more profitably / Jeff Koser & Chad Koser. -- 1st ed.

    p. : ill. ; cm.
    Includes index.
    ISBN: 978-1-929774-57-9

1. Sales management--Handbooks, manuals, etc. 2. Selling--Handbooks, manuals, etc. 3. Sales personnel--Handbooks, manuals, etc. 4. Sales personnel--Training of. I. Koser, Chad. II. Title.

HF5438.4 .K67 2008
658.8/1   20089339979

Printed in the United States of America on acid-free paper

08 09 10 11 12 13 14   10 9 8 7 6 5 4 3 2 1

First Edition

CONTENTS

THE ZEBRA WAY

ZERO IN ON YOUR ZEBRA

PARTNER WITH YOUR ZEBRA

CATCH YOUR ZEBRA

THE ZEBRA WAY

CHAPTER 1

HUNTING ZEBRAS

EVER HAD A NICE FAT BONUS—THE KIND that makes your year? Want more just like it? If you haven't had one, don't you want one? Well, we can tell you how to make it happen. It's as simple as changing how and where you spend your time and resources.

First, ask yourself, "How often do I spend time on prospects that are long shots?" If you're like most salespeople, your answer is probably "pretty often." The simple truth is that salespeople work hard to get the business they score, but many of the hardest-working people in sales are the least successful. This reality exists because most salespeople believe that the only way to close more sales is to pursue every opportunity for every possible prospect. That approach isn't effective in the current business environment. Here's a wake-up call.

WAKE-UP CALL

- The most competitive company in an industry closes about 15 percent of its forecasted sales, and its competitors close another 15 percent.

- 70 percent of the prospects in an industry—the sales everybody is fighting for—will never buy from anyone.

- Sales, marketing, sales engineers, customer service, sales management, and lots of other employees waste 85 percent of their time on activities that will never result in a sale.

- Calls from salespeople waste a prospect's energy 85 percent of the time, too.

So why are sales teams spending time developing and executing activity-intensive sales techniques to reach prospects who, 85 percent of the time, will not buy? Why do so many salespeople waste time and energy on something that will never produce the desired result? Because the traditional model of sales management is driven by the philosophy that all sales activity is good activity. Do your sales goals look like this?

Talk with 100 prospects in order to
- Get 25 appointments, so you can . . .
- Do 12.5 prospect surveys, which will lead to . . .
- About 6.25 proposals, and ultimately to . . .
- One sale

If so, you're operating with an activity-driven sales philosophy. Don't fret, you are not alone! The majority of the sales world is still preaching and practicing the activity-driven approach. The end result of building your sales strategies around this worn-out philosophy is that valuable sales time and resources are wasted 85 percent of the time. You need to consider a new approach.

In many ways, salespeople are like lions. Lions need sharp focus to catch enough food to survive, but not all lions hunt the same way. Unlike experienced, disciplined lions, young lions often fail to focus on prey that they can catch and that will effectively feed the pride. They'll take a swipe at any food source within sight, often to no avail, and then pursue another and another until all their energy is spent and they have to abandon the hunt. Like a good salesperson, however, the experienced lion knows that the better strategy is to focus on prey that is worth the energy to pursue, like a zebra.

In a typical year, most salespeople in our complex business environment work a limited number of opportunities. So, spending time and money on an unqualified prospect can be a tremendous drain on a company. When salespeople pursue every opportunity that catches their attention, they exhaust their limited resources until they have nothing left to continue the hunt. Ultimately, even the business that could have been won is often lost, making survival in the wild world of sales increasingly difficult.

When you pursue every opportunity, you exhaust your limited resources until you have nothing left to devote to the best opportunities.

There was a time when more activity produced greater results, but too much has changed to make that approach workable. There are more competitors in every industry, and they have better access to information. They figure out your strengths and work hard and fast to emulate them. Prospects are now saying that it's hard to distinguish between different options. To most prospects, everyone in the market looks the same, and many of the competitive differences that companies *can* claim don't seem to matter. As products begin to appear equal, price becomes more important to customers. Margins have been bled from many industries because India, China, and other developing countries are creating downward price pressure. Their low-cost development and manufacturing resources contribute to the lowest-cost game. Sales are lower, margins are lower, and there is more competition than the market can support.

It doesn't matter if you sell tangible or intangible products and services, large- or small-ticket items: *the activity-based sales approach no longer works!* Sales can no longer be a numbers game. Old-school methods targeting sheer volume of leads and knocking on every door with equal vigor have been proven vastly ineffective, not to mention expensive. Effort alone is no longer enough to be competitive. If effort is the key to your strategy, you will go hungry. Instead of chasing anything that moves, why not hunt zebras? It's time to heed the old cliché about working smarter, not harder.

 Effort alone is not enough to be competitive. If effort is the key to your strategy, you will go hungry.

THE ZEBRA

How would it feel if you could spend more time pursuing prospects that you knew you could win? How would it feel to spend time with those prospects where it matters most—at an executive level? How would it feel if you could get home on time at night and be more involved with family and friends? If you are like most salespeople and you waste 85 percent of your energy on prospects that are poor fits for your product or service, company, or sales strategy, your best chance to improve your sales, build a stable of happy customers, and have a life outside of work is to find your Zebra and develop a method for selling to it.

Your Zebra is the prospect that is a perfect fit for your company—and not just from a product or solution perspective. It is a prospect that you know you can win based on identifiable, objective characteristics—and Zebras are the only prospects a salesperson should pursue. We call this perfect prospect a Zebra because once you've identified the characteristics of your Zebra, you can quickly and easily spot it amid all the other prospects. A Zebra's stripes tell you exactly what kind of animal you're looking at—you can't mistake a Zebra for any other animal, so you know for sure when you have one.

Most good salespeople have an instinct for Zebras. You know in your gut when you've found a prospect that offers you a good chance. It's the perfect prey, and the time and money you spend pursuing this prospect are going to pay off. But you still pursue lots of prospects that aren't Zebras because you believe that if you work hard enough, you can close those deals, too. This is a fallacy that most salespeople believe.

Here's the problem. These companies or individuals may or may not buy from someone, but they aren't going to or shouldn't buy from you. The reason? Their needs don't line up with what your company delivers. You can chase them all you want, but you'll never be able to deliver the solution that meets their needs. If you're focused on pursuing anything other than Zebras, you're just chasing whatever happens to step into view. And putting your energy toward the wrong focus is just as detrimental to sales success as being unfocused.

WAKE-UP CALL

Many great sales authors have devoted text to the importance of profiling your market niche and have helped establish why every company needs a Zebra. Yet most companies agree that although this strategy is generally best, they fail to live by it.

Part of the reason you pursue less-than-ideal prospects is because you can't articulate what makes a Zebra a Zebra. You may instinctually recognize it, but you can't develop a sales strategy based on your Zebra because you don't really understand what it looks like. You haven't identified your Zebra's unique stripes.

If we know that we want to pursue Zebras, why not take the sales process out of the realm of instinct and chance and approach it with direction and discipline? The purpose of this book is to help you do exactly that by showing you how to find your Zebra and how to develop a sales methodology specifically suited to catching the Zebra. We will teach you how to identify Zebras and earn the right to spend time with them at the executive level so that your time is spent where you have the best possible chance of closing the sale—with the decision maker. And we'll show you how the results of using the Zebra methodology go far beyond improved sales.

By focusing only on Zebras it is possible to close as much as 90 percent of the business in your sales pipeline. As a result, you will have greater sales success than you imagined possible, and your life will be richer, more exciting, and more personally rewarding. Want to earn that big bonus again? Learn to identify conventional "sales wisdom" that has sent you chasing after other animals in the past and you can eliminate those fruitless pursuits, freeing up the bulk of your time to spend on Zebras.

WAKE-UP CALL

You may think that if you pursue only Zebras, you'll risk selling less than you are now. It's true that when you first start focusing on Zebras, your potential sales pipeline will decrease in overall value. *But if you're closing 90 percent instead of 15 percent, this short-term discomfort will be worth it.* And because you won't be wasting time on prospects that will never buy from you, you'll have more time to pursue quality accounts where you add unique value. You'll have time to strategize the accounts that are worth your valuable time and sales resources. You'll be able to review your Zebras, determine and leverage your strengths, and identify and devise strategies to address your weaknesses. This is the real strength of the Zebra way. *The more you identify and chase Zebras, the faster the deals in your pipeline will turn into revenue, the less discounting will be required to close business, and the faster your business will grow.*

WHY YOU NEED THE ZEBRA

Making the changes necessary to follow the Zebra way may require a major catalyst for some of you—but if you wait that long, it may be too late. We'll share a true story to help you see how a real person (names have been changed) developed the will and the method to change and overcome a catastrophe. We'll return to our story frequently throughout the book to help you understand how the concepts and tools presented have been used in the real world.

Kurt Kustner is a vice president of operations for the supply-chain solutions division of C3, a conglomerate. Kurt and C3 are the perfect example of why the Zebra is so necessary in the current business environment. Kurt's quota has grown so large and seemingly unachievable that even though he knows it doesn't work, he feels forced to chase every prospect that moves. Still, he is not making his numbers.

Early one morning, Kurt enters his office and finds that his boss, Scotty, has driven up from headquarters and is sitting behind his desk. Scotty looks up when Kurt enters. "Sit down, Kurt." Kurt knows this can't be good. "Last night, I got a call from Mark Nem." Mark Nem is the CEO of Nem's, a plumbing and fixture manufacturer that has been buying products and services from Kurt for several years. Kurt's stomach churns. "Mark told me that we've lost his business."

"Really?" is the best response Kurt can manage to Scotty's dismal news. "Okay, Scotty, this is bad, but I have other ways of getting to my number this quarter," he offers, knowing that it isn't true.

Kurt's division has been working to respond to a request for proposal (RFP) from Nem's. He believes Nem's is the key to meeting his sales numbers for the quarter, so he has been pouring every possible resource into the opportunity. During the sales cycle he involved research and development and the best sales engineering expertise C3 has. But an outside consultant for Nem's wrote the specifications for the RFP, and they didn't align with C3's strengths. Kurt knew he was in trouble as soon as he received the RFP.

"Kurt, you've had a string of bad months. If you can't even bring in the Nem's account, maybe I made a mistake promoting you."

"Wait a minute, Scotty. Take it easy. I know Nem's is an important account, but what's got you so upset?"

Scotty explains that Mark Nem felt that he had allowed C3 every opportunity to continue to earn his business, but Mark's people were disappointed with C3's recent work. C3 had hit them with invoices for even slight alterations to original project specifications. Scotty had defended C3 and countered that the brutal negotiation and low-cost competition had removed most, if not all, of the profit from the original order, so C3 had no choice but to charge for all changes in the project specs.

Mark also complained that C3 had not properly trained Nem's employees on the new system. After C3 confirmed that Nem's employees misunderstood the new solution, C3 requested that Nem's employees undergo additional training. Nem's said that if more education was required, C3 must bear the expense. C3 balked, and the end result was an unhappy customer.

"Mark told me that some of his people didn't even want us included in the short list of providers to receive the latest RFP. We've been doing business with Nem's for a long time, Kurt. Why can't you win even when you have the advantage?"

"Scotty, you've cut our sales engineering staff and eliminated customer-service personnel. I'm lucky to have closed *any* business recently."

Scotty slams a hand on the desk. "Don't cry to me about not having enough people. You need to look at the low number of prospect calls, surveys, demonstrations, and proposals you're doing—or should I say, not doing! Your team's activity levels are low, Kurt, and you know it." Scotty stands up and closes the door. Considering that no one else is even in the office, Kurt knows this isn't good.

"Losing Mark Nem's business is just a symptom of larger problems. Do you think I would drive up here at this hour just to talk about the Nem's order?" Scotty pauses and gives Kurt a hard look. "I came here to tell you that you have ninety days to show progress, or we'll start more layoffs ... and one of them will be you."

Feeling exhausted, Kurt asks, "What do you want me to do?"

"Kurt, I hired you because I thought you could build some momentum and turn things in a positive direction. I still believe that, but you've got to improve your activity levels if we're going to have a chance."

Scotty gets up to leave, offering one more bit of bad news on his way out the door. "We're having an emergency sales meeting at nine o'clock on Saturday at headquarters. Everyone's required to be there."

Kurt sits down at his desk, reflecting on his current situation. Hard work had always solved sales problems in the past. But now it seems he has been working harder and putting more hours in than ever before for less results. What is he going to do? *Scotty is right about one thing, Kurt thinks. The problem isn't that the Nem's order went away. The problem is larger than one single order. But the answer can't be more mindless, resource-wasting activity.*

Can you feel Kurt's stomach churn? Will it take a catastrophic event like Kurt's before you consider a change? Obviously, his boss, Scotty, is devoted to the activity-based sales approach, and Kurt is right to question the drive for activity as a solution to their problems. Kurt's situation may be familiar to some of you. And if it isn't, it might be in the near future if you aren't considering new ways of doing business—new ways of addressing your critical sales issues.

The most successful salespeople in the world have something in common: they know how to identify and address their critical sales issues. Do you know what your critical sales issues are? Could you make a list right now, without too much thought or analysis? If you're like most salespeople, your list will probably look like this:

 WAKE-UP CALL

- Sales cycles are getting longer and often end with no decision—they just linger in limbo.

- Qualified prospects are difficult to find and identify—your pipeline is clogged.

- Sales opportunities are aging and staying on the forecast longer—and time kills all deals.

- Products and services are becoming increasingly commoditized—prospects are saying, "All products and solutions look alike."

- Deals are getting smaller and margins are diminishing—heavy discounting is the norm.

- Access to high-level decision makers is harder to get—the number of competitors in every market is on the rise.

If you are facing these hurdles, you're not alone. Every client we've worked with has been affected by at least one of these issues. And increasing sales activity doesn't help a company address them. By focusing on activity rather than productivity and overcoming critical sales issues, sales teams are burning through dwindling resources and having a tougher time making their numbers.

Some of the wasted effort in sales is a consequence of the fact that most sales are initiated by a prospect, often with a request for proposal (RFP) or a request for information (RFI). As salespeople we expend much of our energy keeping ourselves involved in the competition of customer-initiated and customer-driven sales cycles where we never had a chance to win in the first place. We feel we must respond, and we do so without fully qualifying the opportunity, considering the resources we're expending to pursue it, or evaluating how likely it is that we'll win the business.

Additionally, large, hot prospects are often allowed to change R&D priorities. As a result, R&D teams can never finish new product releases on time because the sales staff is always bringing in the next big opportunity, changing their priorities. R&D is whipsawed around, missing deadlines, and credibility suffers. Sales fall behind the competition, and a chain of events has begun that will result in closing even less business in the future.

Another element that has pulled our attention toward activity levels and away from results is the advent of customer relationship management (CRM) systems. The proliferation of CRM systems has automated the collection and analysis of data, which makes it easy to generate reports on sales activity. The activity that we enter into CRM systems falsely encourages us, implying that we're productive simply because our activity levels are high. Problematically, companies and individuals end up using CRM systems to measure the quantity of sales activity rather than the quality, requiring salespeople to spend countless hours logging the quantitative data. But CRM systems also offer the benefit of collaboration and the ability to measure actual progress and productivity; unfortunately, most companies do not take advantage of this asset. Using the Zebra model in conjunction with a solid CRM can actually help you identify and overcome your sales hurdles.

Putting sales activity quantity ahead of quality generally yields a very poor return on investment (ROI) within both sales and business-development departments. Available people resources are torn in many directions by the sales department. There's such a push to attain the required activity levels that salespeople fail to focus that activity where it truly matters. As a result, there is little time left to actually work the deals that should be won; resources are scattered in many directions rather than concentrated on only the most viable opportunities.

With the Zebra model, you'll have the information you need to decide to pull out of unfavorable cycles and respond with full energy to those opportunities that fit your Zebra profile. Wouldn't that be a great way to do business?

All of this pointless activity not only prevents focus on the most important sales issues but also leads to further problems down the line. When we pursue opportunities that aren't a good fit for us and somehow actually win the business, we often end up sacrificing quality and margins and adding to the list of unhappy customers.

 WAKE-UP CALL

When you sell to customers who shouldn't be buying your solution or product, you end up with

- High discounting that results in low margins
- Lack of knowledge of the customer's business and industry
- An ineffective plan for implementation
- Post-implementation customer problems that drain company resources
- Poor reputation in the market

And how does this intense focus on activity over productivity affect the inner workings of a company? Usually it results in poor-quality sales proposals, unrealistic timelines for everybody involved in the sale, low morale as more employees are forced to deal with the issues of unhappy customers, and less time to think and act strategically because everybody's focus is on managing crises.

These are the problems Kurt is wrestling with on Saturday morning at headquarters while he's waiting for the meeting to start. It's 9:00 A.M., and instead of enjoying breakfast with the family or helping his son prepare for his Little League game, Kurt is sitting in a conference room with the leaders of other C3 divisions. Everybody was told to bring the usual activity reports, pipeline close rates, and so on, but they don't know what the meeting is about. They're expecting another push to increase activity levels, though, and Scotty doesn't disappoint.

"Sales activity levels are down across the company," Scotty admonishes. "Even yours are low, Kent!" The disappointment in his tone startles everyone. Kent Clark's team has close rates that are the highest in the company—by a lot.

"But your sales numbers seem to be way up . . . that just can't be." Scotty seems almost suspicious of the results in front of him. Ignoring the data that don't support *his* viewpoint, he continues. "Here are the new activity levels and expectations. They'll be available the next time you log on to Bertha."

Bertha is a CRM system Scotty had installed last year; it keeps him on top of the latest sales activity statistics. The sales teams named the CRM "Bertha" because they view it as large, unyielding, unforgiving, and ready to bite you if you don't do as instructed. Scotty doesn't realize that's the general opinion in the company. The system was intended to help the company work large deals more efficiently, seamlessly, and collaboratively across the organization. But although Bertha does provide a means for collaboration and does help management with what they think they need, it has not helped move sales in a positive direction. Activity-level data are always available at the touch of a button, however, and that pleases Scotty very much.

"The answer is clear to me," Scotty says in closing. "We've got to improve our sales efficiency. To do that, we have to drive sales activity. Additional prospect mailings, sales calls, customer meetings, demonstrations, and proposals are the best tactics to work our way out of our present situation. To spike this activity drive, we will *all* participate in a five-thousand-piece prospect mail campaign."

Kurt groans internally, knowing that a mail campaign isn't going to make a difference.

The meeting finally ends, and everybody looks discouraged. As Kurt leaves the building, he runs into Kent and asks him if he wants to share a cab to the airport. He wants to find out how Kent's sales numbers have become so high.

They get into a taxi and exchange updates on their families. Then Kurt gets down to business. "Kent, you have to tell me what your secret is. I don't want to sound like Scotty, but how are your sales so high if your activity levels are low? Is Bertha doing something for you that she isn't doing for me?"

"Let me ask you a couple of questions, Kurt. Who's your most active salesperson?"

"Probably Gill. And Gill is religious about recording all of his activity in Bertha."

"And how is Gill doing on his quota right now?"

"He's only at about 20 percent."

"And who's your least active salesperson?"

"Well, I guess that would be Jim Steelburg, at least on paper."

"And where is he on quota?"

"He's doing great. In fact, he's already over 100 percent for the year."

"Exactly. My group found that our best salespeople are often the least active in Bertha. They realize it's quality, not quantity, that really counts. I'm not saying that it's always the case, but often the salespeople who are the least productive against quota are the most current and active in Bertha."

"Hmm . . . interesting. Unfortunately, Scotty wants to see activity, and he doesn't seem to listen when I try to talk to him about real productivity." Kurt sighs, thinking about the new push for activity.

"Yeah, well, that's Scotty," Kent snorts.

"What other gems have you got?"

"Have you heard about our Zebra?"

Just then the cab pulls up to Kent's terminal at the airport. "I've got to catch my flight," Kent says as he jumps out of the cab. "Let's talk next week and I'll share some more info with you."

"Sounds great," Kurt replies, feeling hopeful about his work for the first time in a long time, yet for a reason he can't exactly identify.

We'll return to Kurt's story throughout the book to explore how the way of the Zebra can be implemented even in a company that is devoted to the activity-based approach, and how that change can result in less wasted energy and resources, shorter sales cycles, improved access to decision makers, better margins, and increasing sales.

WAKE-UP CALL

Measuring activity—even on poorly qualified opportunities—may make you feel like you're getting somewhere, but if you don't close the deal, isn't it just wasted effort anyway? Counting and monitoring the small, activity-based successes is a good way to justify a CRM system, but it isn't necessarily going to reveal how successful you'll be at closing the prospects you're working on—unless you begin by measuring the right prospects. Most sales managers argue that you can't predict prospects that will turn into revenue except to count the steps to success, which is why they measure activity. But there really is a better way. By evaluating each prospect against your Zebra profile (we'll help you create it!) and against those prospects you've closed in the past, you can more accurately predict future sales success. And we're going to show you just how easy it is to do!

THE ZEBRA BUYING CYCLE

As you can tell from our story, Kurt is dealing with some serious sales issues. Without a change in behavior—and, more importantly, without results—our Kurt is no longer going to have a job. Identifying C3's Zebra will help focus his sales efforts and resources and dramatically increase his pipeline close rates, but it won't help him address all of the problems that are affecting his division. Kurt needs more than a Zebra—he needs a different sales approach.

If you follow the way of the Zebra and apply analysis, process, focus, and discipline, this results-driven approach will offer greater reward with less work. To help you do this, we've developed the Zebra Buying Cycle. We use the phrase *buying cycle* rather than the traditional *sales cycle* for good reason. A sales cycle is named as such because traditionally the salesperson seeks someone to sell to. The Zebra Buying Cycle process targets the person who is going to buy from you—the person with decision-making power who defines the company's business issues, who is responsible for the promises that will get the project approved and for achieving and reporting the end results. We call this person Power.

 WAKE-UP CALL

You should be selling to Power because Power

- Defines the company's business issues
- Is responsible for project promises
- Approves projects
- Is responsible for results

When Power is presented with a solution that addresses key pain points, he or she has the authority to make the decision to buy! So another critical element of the Zebra Buying Cycle is identifying the pain points needed to reach Power and make the most of your time and resources. Why waste your time selling to someone who doesn't want your solution or doesn't have the authority to buy?

 Why waste your time selling to someone who doesn't want your solution or doesn't have the authority to buy?

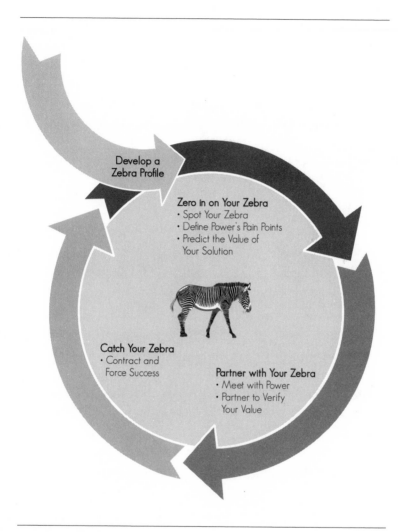

The Zebra Buying Cycle

The figure shown here represents the preliminary step of developing a Zebra profile and the three stages of the Zebra Buying Cycle. One thing we can promise you is that this process is different from anything you have ever tried. Some of the differences are subtle; some are not so subtle. First, you are selling to Power, and Power, unlike lower-level managers, is paid to evaluate risk, make decisions based on that risk, and carry out a plan of action in support of those decisions. Second, the process enables you to give Power everything she needs to make a decision in the shortest possible time. During the cycle, you'll give Power information that

- Predicts very specifically the value she can expect to achieve
- Makes the decision-making process easy
- Describes the best process for evaluating your solution and what it will take in terms of time and resources
- Clearly explains what her company will lose by not moving forward with your solution.

GET READY FOR AMAZING RESULTS

The Zebra and the Zebra Buying Cycle are designed to help you answer the three most important sales questions quickly, easily, and consistently:

- Will this prospect buy anything?
- Will this prospect buy from me?
- Will this prospect buy now?

And when you follow the Zebra way, you can expect to

- Increase your pipeline close rates
- Shorten sales cycles
- Increase the average deal size
- Increase sales to new and existing clients

- Reduce discounting and increase margins
- Make better use of your scarce resources
- Make all of your customers happy and reference worthy
- Solve other sales pain points specific to your business

Most importantly, though, we won't just give you theories and concepts. We'll give you specific tools, models, and spreadsheets that you can customize and use to apply the Zebra profile and the Zebra Buying Cycle to your business. These are the tools we've developed for our clients, and we're going to give them to you free of charge! (Don't you hate it when people say that?) Well, ours are almost free. You did buy this book, after all, and you'll have to work to turn the templates into valuable, viable tools for your specific business. The templates are free, but combined with your knowledge, they'll become priceless.

In the following sections of the book, we'll take you through the step-by-step process of how to identify, sell to, and close your Zebra. You will learn how to determine the Power pain points your solution addresses and uncover the value your solution creates. You'll use information about your product to create a foolproof model that will predict and prove the value you'll create for your Zebra. We will give you specific information that will help you secure appointments with Power and create custom presentations that reflect your unique message. We'll describe the process for proving the value that can be achieved with your solution. Finally, you'll learn how to negotiate for the business and force the success of the solution to create a happy, long-term customer.

Why leave it to intuition and chance when there is a foolproof, easy, completely developed method at your fingertips?

If you can imagine the benefits of leveraging the Zebra model to improve your sales and get to the people who have the power to make a buy decision, then you've taken the first important step. Why leave it to intuition and chance when there is a foolproof, easy, completely developed method at your fingertips? Read on to discover and create all of the tools you need to change your sales productivity and your life.

CHAPTER 2

DEVELOP YOUR ZEBRA PROFILE

"OKAY, SO NOW WHAT?" YOU'RE PROBABLY ASKING. "This Zebra thing sounds great in theory, but how do we actually figure out what our Zebra looks like?" Well, we're going to show you, and this part of the process is fun and interesting. You get to revel in the glory of your sales wins and your host of happy customers.

You see, a Zebra is more than just solution fit, more than just business needs, more than just willingness to buy. A Zebra is the perfect sales prospect, and that means your Zebra is a combination of all of these things and more. You probably already recognize this in your best customers, but how do you apply this knowledge to your prospects? You likely don't. And that's why you need a Zebra profile.

The Zebra profile outlines the characteristics of those companies that represent your best opportunities. It is the best tool for quickly, easily, and accurately identifying the Zebras among your prospects—without relying on gut instinct. First, let's take a closer look at what a Zebra is.

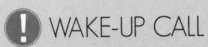

! WAKE-UP CALL

A Zebra is a perfect sales prospect:

- A Zebra's business needs match the promised benefits of your company's solution.
- A Zebra fits with your company philosophically, demographically, politically, and culturally.
- A Zebra likely buys the way *you* sell.
- A Zebra allows you access to Power.
- A Zebra is ready to buy if the return on investment is right.
- A Zebra is the sum of the company, operational, technology, and service characteristics that define your best customers.

If you are selling correctly—and that means working with Power—you should be able to close deals with your Zebras 90 percent of the time, but it's going to take some work to get there. To follow the Zebra way, you have to go beyond the relatively basic traditional techniques of customer and prospect analysis to find patterns in the way your best customers and prospects do business. Rather than simply considering what your target prospects say, you'll focus on how they behave. You'll find patterns in the way they shop for and purchase a solution, the way they buy from others, and the overall way they conduct business.

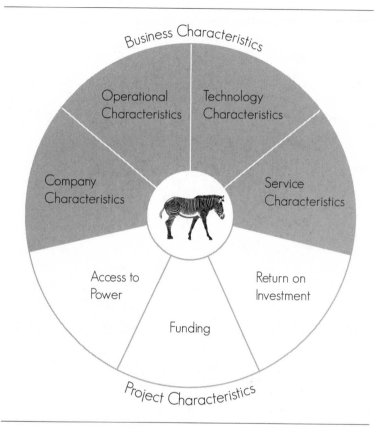

The Zebra Characteristics

 If you are selling correctly, you should be able to close deals with your Zebras 90 percent of the time.

By focusing on your prospects' size, culture, industry vertical, source of decision-making power, and overall look and feel, you'll be able to sell far beyond features, functions, and even solutions to determine a mutually beneficial fit. When you learn how to identify and sell to Zebras, you'll dig all the way into your prospects' core values. Then you can look at—and sell—solution fit, but not from a typical feature or function perspective. Instead, we'll teach you a better approach: to analyze solution fit from the perspective of the customer's business issues—Power's pain points. Determining and selling to these pain points is absolutely critical to your success because they are what drive decision-making behavior. We'll show you how to do it starting in chapter 4. But it only works if you're actually pursuing a Zebra, so you have to do the legwork first.

Kurt is doing some legwork of his own a few days after the meeting at headquarters. He's trying to address an important problem: not enough resources to cover his expansive, but weak, pipeline. So he's talking to the manager of presales consultants, Dave, to understand why that team never seems to be able to satisfy prospects' requests on time and keeps missing deadlines.

"Dave, do we have your team working on projects we don't have a chance of winning?"

"Is that a trick question?" Dave replies with an incredulous look.

"No. I want an honest answer."

"You know I work on projects all the time where I don't think we fit," Dave says. "You, the sales managers, and the sales reps all think every opportunity can be turned around. You say that if you 'smother an account,' you'll win it. The problem is that we can smother only a few deals at a time."

"Yeah, we are guilty of that approach, aren't we? . . . I am guilty of that," Kurt states more affirmatively.

Dave then explains that he has spent the past two weeks working on one large project and overseeing the presales efforts on all the other major deals, including several where C3 is not a strong fit. The latter prospects won't let C3 simulate the solution or use their engineering strength and material-flow expertise to solve known supply-chain business issues, simply because the issues aren't referenced in the specifications or requested in the RFP. Dave concludes with the most egregious consequence of this approach: because C3 has spent so much time on low-probability opportunities, they now risk losing a prospect for which they have an excellent fit. "OMI allowed us to help write the specifications for their RFP," Dave says. "They paid us to review their business requirements and create a specification. But now our largest competitor has pushed its way through the door, mostly because we haven't been able to finish our work and have delayed returning the final results. With all the other activity we're spread out on, we just haven't had time to work on what's truly important."

Kurt feels queasy as he thanks Dave for the input and picks up the phone to call Kent Clark. He's hoping that Kent can expand on the discussion they started in the cab and give him some feedback on how to solve his sales problems.

"Hey, Kurt," Kent says cheerily when he hears Kurt's voice on the other end of the line. "How've you been?"

"Frustrated and curious," Kurt replies. "I've thought a lot about activity versus productivity, but haven't come up with any solutions to my quota problem. But I get the impression you've got a solution, so tell me about this Zebra you mentioned."

"Well, the reporting of sales activity doesn't really have anything to do with increasing sales, does it?"

"No, I don't think so."

"And has more activity helped you increase your pipeline close rates?" Kent asks.

"Clearly not," Kurt replies, thinking about what Dave said. "I'm starting to think it may have actually hurt us."

"Well, how would it feel if you could spend more time on real prospects where it matters most—at an executive level? How would it feel if you could get home on time at night and see your kids more? How would it feel if you could do all of this and increase your close rate to meet your quota?" Kent baits Kurt with questions that have an obvious answer.

"It would feel great. So how can I make that happen?" Kurt pushes, beginning to lose patience.

"About twelve months ago, I started to think about my customer base in terms of which customers I was using as references, and I found a pattern that should have been obvious. My best customers were my best references. It sounds so simple and silly, but it made even more sense once I started to dissect what makes a good customer. Then I analyzed which customers were the best from a repeat-business and profitability perspective. Again, just as you would expect, my most reference-worthy customers were continuing to buy more from me, and at a higher margin," Kent says.

Kurt interrupts. "Kent, C3 marketing has done a good job of figuring out how our product fits our prospects operationally and what problems we help them solve; therefore, where we should spend our time. Is that what you're talking about here? What's different about your approach?"

"What's different is that this time I went beyond the techniques we've always used, and I started to see critical patterns and similarities in my best customers. I even created a cross-functional team to help us learn more about the characteristics of our best customers. I included salespeople, sales engineers, customer service, and execs from marketing, legal, and even human resources.

"I discovered that my best customers, like us, are highly quality focused. My best customers allow us to sell to our own strengths—they buy the way we sell. We are allowed to study the business problem, engineer a solution, simulate that solution, and configure all of the pieces needed to make them successful.

"I spent time determining which customer technology issues created competitive differentiation for our solution, and which technology issues created challenges when compared with competing solutions. I also looked at our service offerings and how they fit into our best customers' expectations and needs.

"When I was done, I had created the profile of my perfect customer. I had assessed our best customers, each of our recent sales wins, and even our most recent losses. Ultimately, I used this information to create my profile of the perfect prospect, or what we've started calling a Zebra."

"Why a Zebra?" Kurt asks.

"Well, I know when I am looking at a zebra that it's a zebra. There is no mistaking it for any other animal. With this profile, my best prospects are now just that clear. Good salespeople seem to have a sixth sense to know when they're going to win, and I think I have that. But the reality is that sometimes I need specific direction or real analysis to rely on because I also believe that given enough time, I can win any deal. And we all know that too much time on any one deal eventually kills all deals—for all salespeople, and in all businesses. Listen, I've got to run to a meeting, Kurt, but I'll send you some information about my Zebra and we can talk more later in the week."

"Thanks, Kent. I really appreciate you sharing this with me." Kurt hangs up with a smile on his face, already thinking about his best customers and what their stripes look like.

The materials that Kurt received from Kent revealed that Kent had analyzed his customer base in terms of seven attributes:

- Company characteristics
- Operational characteristics
- Technology characteristics
- Service characteristics
- Access to Power
- Funding
- Return on investment

We'll explore each of these seven categories and how they create the foundation of a Zebra profile, but first you need to understand how to go about creating a Zebra profile.

THE ZEBRA TEAM

The first step you must take toward creating a Zebra profile is to pull together your Zebra team. The information gathering and analysis required in the Zebra process should involve input from a variety of departments. It's important to include all of the major functional areas of your business in the creation of your Zebra because they may have insights that you would not consider. For instance, the legal department may have important points to make about negotiations with your best customers. Human resources may have input on staffing changes necessary to better support the actual needs of your Zebras, or they may need to be alerted to changes in how you will be hiring salespeople in the future based on the Zebra methods. And in the end, the creation of your Zebra will affect everybody in the company.

If you begin focusing on meeting the needs of your Zebra from a cross-departmental perspective, soon you'll have the entire organization working on prospects, and subsequently customers, where you bring quantifiable superior value. The process will galvanize your entire organization. Everyone will speak the same language and will have a strong understanding and commitment to creating happy customers.

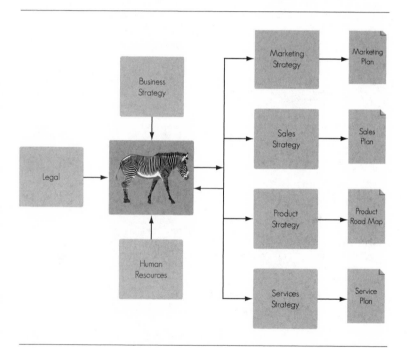

Collaborating to Create Your Zebra Profile

WAKE-UP CALL

Creating a Zebra profile for your business is interesting and rewarding. You'll need the following resources to do it right:

- The time and energy of the leaders of various departments
- Information about the inner workings of your best customers, including why your products have been purchased and what value they have achieved. (We'll present some good information-gathering techniques in chapters 4 and 5 that might be useful in this process)
- Information from various departments about the working relationships with your customers
- Publicly available data on the financials for each customer
- A clear understanding of why you won recent new business and why you lost recent opportunities

THE SOURCE OF YOUR ZEBRA PROFILE: YOUR BEST CUSTOMERS

Finding companies that are your Zebras is all about identifying the types of companies that have a need for the specific things that make your solution compelling versus your competition's. To do this, begin by thinking about your existing customer base in terms of which customers you would use as references, just as Kent did. What makes those customers good references? It sounds intuitive and maybe even simplistic, but once you dissect the traits that make them good customers, you will unlock the key to identifying good prospects to pursue—to finding your Zebras.

Once you have your team in place, the first question to ask is: Which customers are our best in terms of repeat business and profitability? Just as you would expect, your most reference-worthy customers will tend to be those that continue to buy from you, and also provide your business with the greatest profit potential because they typically buy from you at a higher margin.

Next, consider what makes you a good fit with your best customers. Why do you consider them to be your best customers? It is probably a positive relationship on many levels. But what makes it a positive relationship, aside from revenue and margin? This is a question that requires input from all departments that interact with customers on a regular basis. Consider these questions in broad terms initially. We'll talk specifics later.

Next, evaluate recent sales wins, looking for the common threads. Why did you win? What do your new customers say is the reason they bought from you? If you haven't already, ask them, "Why did you buy from me?" Ask now! This will help you understand what your current strengths are in your customers' eyes. And knowing your strengths is the first step to leveraging them.

Although you want to focus on your best customers to define what your Zebra is, it's also important to know what your Zebra is not. This will allow you to quickly assess prospects that are anti-Zebra and eliminate them from your pipeline. Take a look at your most recent sales losses and ask yourself these questions:

- How do the losses differ from your recent wins?
- Which competitor won the business?
- Why did they win?

If you don't know the answers to these questions, you should call the prospect and ask. And don't forget to evaluate deals you worked on that never closed—the limbo prospects. The biggest sales time drain for most companies is apathy—sales cycles that end in no decision.

Once you've compiled a list of your best customers and some basic information about their characteristics, you are ready to begin creating your Zebra Profile using the seven categories (company characteristics, operational characteristics, technology characteristics, service characteristics, access to Power, funding, and ROI). As you work through each characteristic, considering the questions we'll discuss in the rest of the chapter, write down your answers to the questions and any specific patterns you see among these companies. Use these notes to create appropriate qualifying descriptions that comprise both the weakest and the strongest ends of the Zebra spectrum for each category.

Kurt is contemplating this process as he watches people from his division file into the conference room. He has spent the last few days poring over the materials Kent sent, and he thinks he's ready to start sharing these insights with the rest of his division. Kurt knows he has less than ninety days to save himself and his division, so he has to move quickly.

"Okay, everybody, let's get started." All heads in the room turn to him expectantly; nobody knows the purpose of this meeting. "I think most of you have a pretty good understanding of the trouble this division has seen in recent months. And we're pretty far off quota for this quarter already. Do you remember when Scotty was here last week?"

"How could we forget?" sales manager Jennifer asks. "I heard about it in the field before he even left the building."

Kurt takes a big breath and dives in. "His visit was not a social call. He came to tell me we have ninety days to show some progress in our division or we'll be shut down."

Silence falls over the room, and then everyone starts talking at once, firing questions at Kurt. Kurt shares what he knows about the ultimatum, which isn't much. "I know it doesn't seem like a lot of time. It isn't. But until they close us, sell us, or fire me, I'm not giving up. What you decide to do is your business; if you do want out, leave now. For the next three months, I am going to need everything you can give me. If we can show some progress, I'll go all the way to the board to ask for more time."

"Wow," sighs Mike, head of R&D. "I could sense a change in you recently, but I had no idea ... Do you really think we can do enough to make a difference?"

"I do," Kurt says, looking at each member of his team. "I honestly do."

With renewed intensity, Mike asks, "So what can we do?"

"Well, most of you probably know about the successes that Kent Clark's team has had over the past nine months or so." Most people nod their heads. "They've implemented a new system they're calling the Zebra, and I think it might be exactly what we need." Kurt spends some time reviewing what he's learned about the Zebra method so far and what types of results Kent's team has seen, including its distinction as the only C3 division showing any growth. "Kent's team is on fire. They have been selling products, having fun, and getting home at a reasonable hour every night. Sounds interesting and appealing, don't you think?"

Everyone concurs—Dave's voice is louder than all of the rest.

"Well, let's dig into the details then!" Kurt tries to build energy in the room. "Kent's team has been using their business Zebra as the foundational tool for how they approach prospects and sales. So our first step is developing our Zebra. We'll do some research and gather what we consider to be the attributes of the perfect prospect. When we finish, we should have a document that describes in detail our division's Zebra. All opportunities can then be reviewed against the profile before we use any sales resources to pursue them. This way, our eyes are open to all the possible strengths and weaknesses that determine our chances for mutual success with a prospect."

Kurt eyes his staff. "So, for example, let's talk about Nem's. We all knew once the consultant got involved at Nem's that we were in trouble. What did we do about it?"

No one answers.

"Well, the intent of the Zebra process is to identify our strengths and weaknesses in relation to the requirements of a prospect. From there, we can come up with strategies to accentuate our strengths and address our weaknesses. If we had used this process with Nem's, we would have easily identified key frustrations we were not addressing with our sales strategy and approach."

Everyone remains silent, so Kurt proceeds. "We all know getting to the decision maker—Kent's team calls this person Power—early in the sales cycle is critical to success. At Nem's, although we had access to the president, Mark Nem, we didn't leverage this relationship to change the sales cycle in ways that would help both Nem's and us."

"Okay, Kurt, we get the picture," Dave says. "So where do we start?"

"We start by creating a list of our best customers and then answering some questions about them. We also need to analyze

our recent wins and losses. So to start, I want each of you to tell
me who you think our top three customers are and why . . ."

Kurt's team works long into the night. They spend the next few
days going to their customers with questions about the business
relationship to help them refine their information. They work hard
and fast, knowing that their jobs might depend on how well they
can identify which prospects they should be pursuing.

COMPANY CHARACTERISTICS

To assess the company characteristics of your Zebra, first evaluate
your best customers and the last five deals you won by asking yourself some questions about how these companies do business.

- How did these companies behave during the sales cycle?
  Were they open, inviting, honest, and forthright, or was it
  difficult to communicate with them?
- Were contract negotiations smooth and uneventful, or tense
  and tiresome?
- Were you able to position and sell all that you offer?

Next, consider the size of the companies in your set. Are you
selling to small, medium-sized, or large companies? Or is there no
pattern? If size does seem to matter, what are the annual revenues?
If you sell to large companies, do you sell at the corporate or at the
division level?

What are the business philosophies and ideals of your best
customers? Is there something that distinguishes them? For example, how do they feel about quality? Do they have a quality focus,

with less regard for price? Or are cost and availability the traits that helped turn these prospects into customers?

You also must consider how these companies buy from you. The way companies buy from you will change over time as your solution gets more established in the market. One way to think about your customers' buying habits is in terms of the product-adoption life cycle, which depicts five major classifications of buying habits: innovators, early adopters, early majority, late majority, and laggards. Which category best describes the customers who buy from you? Why is this important? Understanding where your customers fit in the product-adoption life cycle can help you refine your sales approach. Keep in mind, though, that selling in the early majority and late majority categories is a very necessary step for survival, as this is where most companies fall.

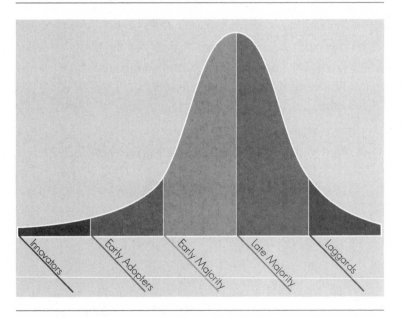

Product-Adoption Life Cycle

Next, ask the question: What is the position of our best customers and recent wins in the marketplace? Are they leaders in their respective markets, or would they best be described as second-tier players?

What are the industries where your solution fits best—retail, pharmaceuticals, healthcare, banking? After you have identified the broad industry groups, the more precise you can be in narrowing them down the better. For example, if you do well in manufacturing, what specific sectors of manufacturing offer your best opportunities for success? To be very specific, it is best to list the Standard Industrial Classification (SIC) codes, or the National American Industry Classification System (NAICS) codes where you have had the most success.

How about location? Where are your best customers located? Does location matter?

After you've considered all of the questions we've presented here and compiled the information, spend some time looking at any other company characteristics that may be relevant to your particular business. What other patterns can you identify?

Kurt's team developed the following company characteristics for their Zebra profile:

Our best customers are profitable, well-branded, stable Global 2000 companies with a strong domestic and international presence. They are

- Metrics-driven. Proof of this characteristic includes use of Six Sigma techniques, a lean initiative, total quality management, or other metrics-driven approaches, or a total-cost-of-ownership focus and philosophy.

• Technology-driven. They believe in what we do. They spend or plan to spend a significant amount on automation.

C3 offers a unique, differentiable solution within each of the following industry markets:

SIC Code	Industry	Percentage
35XX	Machinery	23%
20XX	Food & Beverage	22%
50XX	Distribution	19%
36XX	Electronic equipment	17%
38XX	Instruments	7%
37XX	Transportation equipment	6%
25XX	Furniture	5%
24XX	Wood products	2%

OPERATIONAL CHARACTERISTICS

You've probably always understood the operational characteristics that make a prospect a worthy target; those are easy to identify simply based on what your solution does for the customer. It's easy to discuss how your product fits your prospects operationally and what operational problems you help them solve. These solution-selling techniques have been king in the sales world for years. For your Zebra profile, though, you will need to dig deeper.

But here is the irony of selling to the executive level: We don't lead with operational issues. We lead with higher-level business issues that we will address in chapter 4 when we discuss Power's

WAKE-UP CALL

Do you know where your customers fall in the product-adoption life cycle?

- Innovators and early adopters: buy the newest, most recent, most innovative solutions first, often before the rest of the market is aware a solution is even available; will purchase before complete solutions are available; generally purchase because they are confident they can make your product work with or without you; envision, even better than you, how your product will help them create a competitive advantage for their business. You don't need to position a value proposition to innovators and early adopters because they intuitively realize the value.

- Early majority and late majority: tend to purchase products and solutions once they have been proven; are more pragmatic; need clear explanations of the competitive advantage and vision of your solution; often want and need your assistance during implementation; often are looking for guarantees of success in the form of solid references and testimonials to convince them of the merit of your offering. Success in selling to them will be dependent upon your ability to articulate value. Repeatability and value-based selling are requirements for consistent success with early majority and late majority buyers.

- Laggards: wait to buy until they have no other choice, as dictated by government regulation, necessity to survive, or other dire circumstances.

pain-point business issues. But when we verify our value claim, we do, ironically, circle back to the all-important operational issues our solution addresses.

So what are the strong operational differentiable issues you solve? Do you reduce labor, make a certain group more productive, or increase operational efficiency? What specific operational problems do you solve, and what value does that solution create? We'll teach you how to tie them in to the executive level later.

Next, consider your set of reference companies and ask yourself: What are the organizational structures of those companies? Does organizational makeup seem to matter? If it does, where do these companies fall in the spectrum from simple to complex organizational structure?

- Number of divisions, branches, locations
- Primarily domestic or international
- Owned by a larger corporation, a parent company, or neither

Consider who is responsible for operations and who the end users are in your customer set. Are there patterns in work processes, labor issues, and equipment usage?

Next, consider whether there are patterns in how your customers interact with their external environment. How do they sell their product through to the end customer? Do they have a direct sales force, an indirect channel, independent dealers, or even a two-step distribution process where they sell to someone who sells to someone who ultimately sells to the end customer? How do they interact with suppliers? What types of commitments do they make that relate to your product or solution?

Again, consider any other patterns in operational characteristics that may be relevant to your business.

The operational characteristics of Kurt's Zebra look like this:

C3 customers tend to purchase an updated solution designed to more effectively address supply-chain issues inadequately solved by older solutions. Because they are purchasing solutions as upgrades to existing technology, they are second- or sometimes even third-generation buyers. They want tried-and-true solutions backed up by the proof of success as supplied by many solid references. The more operational complexity that exists within our customers, the more strongly they gravitate to a C3 solution.

- Multi-step distribution and delivery is desirable.
- International and domestic presence adds to the C3 advantage.
- Proliferation of products is causing design and manufacturing slowdown—companies are experiencing growing pains and need an improved supply chain.
- For many customers, the processes for material movement were designed fifteen years ago and no longer fit business requirements prior to the C3 solution being implemented.
- Configure-to-order capabilities are viewed as key to addressing speed to market and competitive differentiation.
- End-of-day or "emergency" shipments require overlapping of shifts, causing unplanned overtime; more automated supply-chain controls could improve this issue.
- Incomplete orders are a common problem that needs to be addressed in order to retain customers and ease production, distribution, and customer service problems.

TECHNOLOGY CHARACTERISTICS

Technology is always a solution differentiator—in any market or industry. To understand your Zebra, you have to know which customer technology issues create a competitive advantage for you and which issues create competitive challenges. An excavation construction company might utilize trucks that each have a global positioning system (GPS) to help them dig and move dirt accurately and avoid hazards. Not all construction companies have this advanced capability; those that do can provide accurate and safe services. If you were a contractor with this capability, you could leverage it for competitive differentiation.

 WAKE-UP CALL

To understand and sell to your Zebra, you have to know the answers to these questions:

- What technology do you offer that adds value for your existing customers?

- What would the ideal scenario be for your best prospects in terms of technology?

- Do you offer a technologically unique solution?

- Do you leverage the technological aspects of your solution to your advantage?

- How do your best customers or recent new customers feel about technology—do they embrace it or run from it?

How a company deals with technology can be uncovered by reviewing the organizational structure. Does the company have a chief information or technology officer (CIO or CTO), or does the highest-ranking technologist have a title like "manager of information technology"? Who does this person report to in the company hierarchy? The answers to these questions will indicate a prospect's technology position. Companies that embrace technology will have a CIO or CTO reporting directly to the CEO or president, and they will probably value solutions that are technologically advanced. If the top-ranking technology executives in your set of companies generally report to the chief financial officer (CFO), your best prospects are technology averse: they view technology as a cost center, not as a strategic resource.

Exploring a company's technology priorities can help you determine if the companies that buy from you are willing to take some calculated risk or if they are generally conservative and tend to play it safe. If they are risk takers, they may be more open to new technology; they may be innovators or early adopters. For example, do your customers tend to utilize open-source software? The open-source movement, in which code is free and available to anyone, is still a pioneering technology strategy, and use of open-source software probably indicates a willingness to take risks. If, on the other hand, your customers play it safe, they are less likely to invest in solutions that incorporate anything other than tried-and-true technology.

For the technology characteristics of your Zebra, you will need to do some further analysis on your own because this category is very dependent on your industry and market. As always, look for patterns in the way your customers approach the technological aspects of your solution, including how the technology affected their decision-making process, the negotiations, the implementation or service, and any other aspect of the buying cycle.

Here is what Kurt's Zebra's technology characteristics look like:

We have a strong technological fit when customer requirements include

- System integration as a key to lowering risk and reducing total cost of ownership
- A preference for using an open "standard" environment such as J2EE, .NET, Java (but not open source)
- A buy philosophy instead of a build philosophy
- The desire for a user-configurable, instead of a customized, solution

We might not have a strong fit when the prospect is dedicated to an open-source environment.

SERVICE CHARACTERISTICS

Most companies consider service as a key differentiator. Most also consider their service personnel to be top in the industry. But being honest with how you compare, and what your customers expect, will help you figure out where you can and should win with prospects.

WAKE-UP CALL

Answer the following questions—and be honest! Compared to your competition,

- What is the depth of your service department?

- How many individuals have been in the business for more than ten years, fifteen years, etc.?

- Do you have a separate call center or center of excellence for first-line support?

- Do you offer varying levels of service contracts?

- Do you keep service quality or uptime statistics?

- What are the statistics supporting your call center measurement?

- What is your policy regarding escalation and the extent of your escalation capabilities?

Now that you've analyzed your service capabilities, you have to match up those capabilities with what your customers expect. What are the service needs and wants of those who have bought from you? Generally, are your best customers do-it-yourselfers, do they need 24/7 service, or are they somewhere in the middle? What level of service did your best customers or recent wins contract for? How did they negotiate on service? Some companies respect and value service and others see it as a necessary evil. Are your best customers historically willing to pay for a guaranteed level of service, or are they willing to accept something less?

Here is what Kurt's service characteristics for his best customers and recent sales wins look like:

C3 service performs strongly when

- Customer covets our ability to install quickly and to reengineer throughout the life of the product; prospects should be focused on quick payback and the process of continuous improvement.
- Customer's philosophy includes the expectation of becoming self-sufficient.
- Customer does not desire extensive field or home office support.

ACCESS TO POWER

Now let's talk about how your past deals have been affected by your access to Power. To analyze this point, you have to know who Power is in the deals you've won and in your best customers. There is no better way to find the real decision maker than to scour the project approval process to find the person who owns the promises and expectations that led to the authorization of the project.

For large critical purchases, Power is usually someone close to and trusted by the CEO. Every company has executives who are counted on to implement the vision of the CEO. These individuals usually have been involved in major projects in the past, so if you are selling a project that is cross-functional and requires a major investment of time and money, look for the executive sponsor of present or past projects that are similar. There might be a lower-level project manager who worked closely with the implementers of the project, but we are looking for the specific executive who set the objectives, oversaw the project, and owned responsibility for delivering upon and reporting progress to the other executives, the CEO, or even the board of directors.

Sometimes Power will be an operations-level individual. This is generally the case for smaller projects or for upgrades or repeat projects.

 WAKE-UP CALL

At the heart of every sales cycle, the decision to buy ultimately comes down to a critical decision maker. Have you been able to identify and gain access to Power on the deals that you've won in the past? Most salespeople don't do a very good job of this. They rely on individuals at the middle-management level to sell their solution up the chain to Power and never meet Power before, during, or after a deal is closed. Power, the key person making the decision to buy from you, is kept out of the loop throughout the majority of the sales cycle. This considered, it would seem that a meeting with Power early on in the buying cycle, as well as continued contact with Power throughout the duration of the buying cycle, is the key to faster, more consistent sales success!

Think about deals you've worked that went smoothly, that closed when and as you predicted they would, and then answer the following questions:

- Who was Power (the real decision maker who chose to buy from you) in those deals?
- What is Power's usual title, and where did he or she fit in the organization?
- Was Power well respected in the organization?
- How would you describe Power's willingness to take risks?
- How would you rate Power in terms of entrepreneurial nature?
- Is Power typically strategic, operational, or more tactical? Why?

Answering these questions will help you determine the Power level you should seek in your prospect accounts and the usual characteristics of Power in your Zebras.

To help you understand the importance of access to Power, look at how your access has differed between your best customers and your worst, between your recent sales wins and losses. For your best customers, did you consistently have access to Power? Who did you actually sell to during the transactions? If you weren't selling to Power, how do you think that affected the sales process and timeline? Asking these questions may help you set a minimum and ideal standard for the people or management levels you'll be willing to sell to in prospect organizations.

FUNDING

Understanding funding, budget issues, and the process of getting financial approval at a prospect company is a key component of understanding your Zebra! Budgets affect every aspect of the buying cycle, and funding issues are often the root of a decision not to buy—from you or at all. You may think it's just a question of

Kurt's team compiles the following description of Power in its Zebra organizations:

- Power is most often a chief operations officer (COO), VP of manufacturing, VP of operations, or VP of logistics. (Less often, Power is an upwardly mobile director of manufacturing, operations or logistics who has strong C-level influence.)
- Power is a highly respected member of the executive team.
- Power purchases from companies that have a well-established reference base.
- Power has a broad solution focus rather than a niche solution focus.
- Power buys our built-to-last approach and expects the useful life of a solution to be more than five years.
- Power is open to conducting a buying process that favors our total solution strengths and the way we sell (i.e., designing a solution, simulation, and complete process flow analysis).

We might be dealing with a non-Power when we are working with a middle manager who is insulated from or keeping us from senior management; true Power will sponsor us to, not block us from, other individuals or areas of the business.

Projects led by purchasing often result in C3 not being permitted to drive a buying cycle that highlights our strengths.

whether they have the money or not, but it's more complicated than that. So, we will continue to talk about the virtues of understanding your prospect's funding process throughout the book—and how that understanding can help you get to Power and close sales.

Many of our past clients have shortened their sales cycles by asking someone in the prospect's finance department to walk them through the process for project approval and funds release. Finance people look at the sales process differently from those in operations. Too often, salespeople solve the operational issues and then run into problems because their operations sponsor doesn't know how to get the project approved and started. Finance always knows. If you have Power on board, Power's sponsorship will give you access to the key people you need in both operations and finance.

When you begin your sales cycles with Power, the budget sometimes becomes less important than it once was because Power often can approve a solution that solves high-level pain points and delivers superior value without even having a budget. And that is exactly where we are going with this process! No self-respecting salesperson should enter into a buying cycle without understanding how funding issues have affected him in the past. So, what is your experience with budgets? Ask yourself: Have our best customers and recent wins had preestablished budgets for our solution? How have funding issues affected our ability to close business, even with our best customers, on a timely basis?

RETURN ON INVESTMENT

Next, we'll address value and the overall return your solution provides. If you haven't developed some type of ROI projection tool for your business, you might not be able to definitively answer the questions we're going to throw at you. But unless you sell primarily

Kurt's team has these comments on funding:

C3 customers tend to budget for a supply-chain solution before they look to purchase. They are conservative buyers primarily in the late majority category of the product-adoption life cycle. For this reason, budget is critical for them.

- They do not buy without a previously approved budget.
- Understanding the capital appropriation review process is key to understanding the C3 Zebra.

Past sales cycles that took considerably longer than normal or that ended in limbo with nondecisions often did so because there was not an approved budget and the sales team could not knowledgeably discuss the prospect's capital approval process.

to innovators and early adopters, you need to be able to communicate to Power the value your solution will create. In chapter 5, we're going to give you the tools to identify and demonstrate your quantifiable value. These tools will change the way you communicate about the value you offer, regardless of your current methods.

Let's look at what type of value your solution or product offers. What specific quantifiable value has your solution created for your best customers or recent sales wins (if you have that information already)? The best type of value is bottom-line or direct value, which is any savings that directly affect profit (the bottom line) for your customer. For example, if your product saves $1 in labor costs (your solution reduces your customer's labor costs by $1), that directly increases profit for your customer by $1. If, instead, you make someone more productive by improving efficiency, your product creates indirect value or indirect savings. Even though your customer's people are able to get more work accomplished, those people will cost the same in terms of wages, benefits, and the like. Finance departments sometimes won't consider indirect benefits when comparing the ROI of similar or even dissimilar projects, so if your product offers only indirect benefits, you'll need to address this issue immediately, before you waste time and resources on a prospect that ultimately will not buy.

Aside from the type of value your product offers, you also need to understand how your best customers have communicated about and perceived that value. Have they required detailed calculations and projections, or have they relied on anecdotal information? Like Kurt's prospects, did they want lots of examples of what you've done for other companies, or were they more interested in how you analyzed their needs and the potential value they could achieve? Luckily for you, the tools we'll give you later in the book will give you everything you need to answer all of your prospects' questions about value and ROI.

There are a lot of ways you could use the information in this chapter. You could take some notes on the questions we recommend you answer about your best customers or recent sales wins and losses. You could take this book to a meeting of your Zebra creation team and use it as a basis for discussion. Regardless of how you use this information, the key is that you come away with a clear understanding of exactly what your Zebra looks like. If the rest of the Zebra method is going to work for you, you first have to have a clear understanding of the differentiable advantage you have over your competition, which the seven characteristics of

Kurt's Zebra profile has these comments on ROI:

- In companies that purchase a C3 solution, Power requires, is involved in, and agrees with the C3 ROI projections.

- Power agrees that other, less expensive solutions won't solve the business problem.

- C3 customers typically require a solution that will last more than five years, so our systems must be built to last.

- Customers recognize that the total cost of ownership of a C3 solution will likely be lower than competitors' and the ROI will be higher, because the C3 solution will require less overall maintenance and upkeep.

your Zebra are designed to identify and accentuate. When you've got that information in hand, you'll be ready for a new, far more effective method of selling.

ZERO IN
ON YOUR ZEBRA

CHAPTER 3

SPOT YOUR ZEBRA

NOW THAT YOU HAVE A CLEAR IDEA of what your Zebra looks like, of who buys from you and why, wouldn't it be great if you could quickly and easily turn that information into sales revenue? Well, do we have the tool for you!

The next step on the Zebra Buying Cycle is to spot your Zebra—determine who your best prospects are and are not by comparing them to your Zebra profile. You've compiled a lot of information about your Zebra, but you have limited information about each of your prospects. So how do you compare and contrast those two sets of information easily, without wasting a lot of time and resources just to discover that a prospect isn't a good fit?

WAKE-UP CALL

The problem with most sales methods or models that sales teams try to implement is that they require too much time to learn or use effectively. Some people may use them, but not everybody. It's just like all the time that's wasted entering details into a CRM system—details that aren't ever going to make a sale happen. Salespeople want to be selling, not crunching data and numbers. They want to know that everything they spend time doing is going to get them closer to a sale. So the best way to make a sales tool useful and used is to make it simple, easy, efficient, and results-oriented. And that's what we've done.

In this chapter, you'll learn how to distill your Zebra profile into just a few statements that describe what makes your solution truly unique, where it fits well, and who would or should buy it. Why simplify? So that you will actually use this technique. Using this simplified information, you will create an analytical tool we call the Push-button Zebra. We'll even give you a downloadable template to use to make it even easier. And by the end of the chapter, you'll understand why all sales reviews should start and end with the strengths and weaknesses of the prospect evaluated against your Zebra profile—and how easy it is to make that happen.

THE PUSH-BUTTON ZEBRA

The Push-button Zebra, or PBZ, is the most effective and efficient way to analyze the prospects in your pipeline. It allows you to quickly and easily identify those prospects that offer you the best opportunity to see a return on your investment of time and resources. And it makes it easy to implement the Zebra process in your organization because it's a tool everybody will be willing to use.

Kurt has finished reading through the Zebra profile he and his team created. There is just one problem. He doesn't think he can get his sales reps to use the Zebra idea because he doesn't know how to take the information and turn it into sales. *Once you pull this information together, how do you use it?* Kurt thinks as he stares at another e-mail from Scotty about activity levels and new ways of reporting them. Feeling a little discouraged and baffled, he calls Kent.

"Hey Kent, it's Kurt," he says when Kent picks up. "We did it. We took the info you sent and we developed our own Zebra profile. My problem is that I don't know how to explain to my team how to turn the profile into improved sales. How do we use it?"

"Yeah, I know all of that information can seem a little daunting. And we know how much salespeople like spending time doing reports," Kent chuckles. "My team struggled with this same question: 'How do we make this easy to use and turn it into relevant information?' So we created a tool we call the Push-button Zebra. Analyzing a prospect is now as easy as pushing a few buttons."

"Okay, this I've gotta hear," says Kurt the skeptic.

"To create the Push-button Zebra, we had to distill the information we'd gathered into a few key points that described the best- and worst-case scenarios for each of the seven attributes in the profile. We then created a grading system for each category to assess where a prospect falls on a scale of 0 to 4. In the end, you get an actual score for the prospect that you can use to decide how to proceed.

"The PBZ allows my team to score prospects pretty easily and make tough decisions quicker," Kent says. "I'm going to send you the PBZ spreadsheet we created. You can fill in your own information. Try it out and let me know what you think."

"Okay, I will," Kurt replies. An ominous question then pops into his head. "Kent, have you talked to Scotty about your Zebra?"

"Well, not exactly. To be honest, I've been able to avoid that discussion for a while now. I've been trying to iron out all of the kinks before I sell it to Scotty. I think I'm going to have to have that conversation soon, though."

Kurt hangs up with Kent and checks his e-mail. There's the spreadsheet Kent promised. As soon as he opens it, Kurt knows he has the tool he needs for his team.

Creating your own PBZ is pretty simple, because you've already done the heavy lifting of creating your Zebra profile. To turn your Zebra profile into a Push-button Zebra, follow these easy steps:

Step 1: For each attribute category of your Zebra profile, identify the most important characteristics of a true Zebra and a true non-Zebra (your worst prospect). These are the characteristics that will immediately let you know if you do or do not have a Zebra in each of the categories. Don't try to distill *all* of your research into twenty or so words. You'll go into more detail in the next step.

Step 2: For each category, create a short description (fifty to seventy-five words) of your Zebra's characteristics. Then develop a brief description of what your anti-Zebra—a very poor prospect fit—would look like. In the PBZ spreadsheet, you can insert these descriptions as comments relating to the brief descriptions you created for each attribute (see the figure on pages 66 and 67 for an example from Kurt's PBZ). This creates a solid foundation for analyzing a prospect.

Step 3: Insert all of this information into the spreadsheet (see the box "The Push-button Zebra Template") and begin scoring prospects!

Shown on the next page is Kurt's PBZ, which he created by plugging the information his team had pulled together for the Zebra profile into the spreadsheet Kent sent to him. The content of this PBZ is very similar to a PBZ we created for a client, so it's a real example of what a PBZ should offer salespeople in terms of information.

The Push-button Zebra Template

To help you create your Push-button Zebra, or just understand the tool better, we've put a sample PBZ Microsoft Excel spreadsheet on our website. Go to www.sellingtozebras.com. Click on "Zebra U," which will take you to the Zebra University page. You'll see a box requesting a user name and password. The box also contains a link that reads "Subscribe to Zebra U." The subscription to Zebra University is free and gives you access to a variety of tools that you can download.

Once you've subscribed and are on the Zebra U website, you'll find a free copy of the Push-button Zebra spreadsheet. Save this spreadsheet to your computer.

When you open it, answer "yes" when it asks if you want to enable macros. Answer "no" when it asks if you want to open the spreadsheet as "read-only." By saying "yes" to enable macros, you are allowing the program that scores the Zebra to run. By saying "no" to open as read-only, you will be able to make changes to this sample Push-button Zebra to create your own PBZ.

C3

ATTRIBUTES FOR ZEBRA SCORE

Prospect Name: Transformers, Inc.

	EXTREMELY UNFAVORABLE				EXTREMELY FAVORABLE	Score	Date	Comment
	0	1	2	3	4			

Company Profile

0	1	2	3	4	Score	Date	Comment
Decisions are all based on price				See value in all of who we are; quality and built-to-last approach valued	4	9/15	Transformers, Inc fits well.

Operations

0	1	2	3	4	Score	Date	Comment
Cherry-pick us; one time there, one time there, or emergency use only				Custom-engineered solutions are required to address difficult needs	3	9/15	Complex requirements, and they know it!

Access to Power

0	1	2	3	4	Score	Date	Comment
Project manager whose only focus is price using a reverse auction				COO or VP of Operations who values our reputation for quality service and a fair price	4	10/1	Have access to controller. Intent is to leverage controller to CFO using the Waterfall Tool

Funding

0	1	2	3	4

Prospect doesn't know funding access steps | Budget criteria established

2

Date	Comment
9/15	Funding verified by controller

ROI

0	1	2	3	4

Not quantifiable | Power agrees with ROI

3

Date	Comment
10/15	Goal is to present to CFO

Technology

0	1	2	3	4

No technology advantage | Prospect values our technology advantage

1

Date	Comment
9/15	

Service

0	1	2	3	4

Tactical; do not value our expertise | Prospect sees us as the experts to be leveraged

1

Date	Comment
11/1	This is still an issue.

18 SCORE

0–9 High Risk	10–19 Some Risk	20–28 ZEBRA

Kurt's Push-button Zebra

While the PBZ is often used to quickly evaluate prospects, and you can get to a Z-score in just a few minutes, it is also a living document. You may have enough information about a prospect to score them low in most attributes and rule them out as a good opportunity right away. More likely, though, you'll have a fair amount of information and you'll do an initial score that is not entirely conclusive. As you progress through the Zebra Buying Cycle and learn more about the prospect, you'll continue to update the PBZ. Before you invest more resources to progress through each stage of the cycle, you'll revisit the PBZ to verify that the prospect is still worthy of pursuit. We'll discuss the scoring process and interpreting the Z-score in more detail throughout the chapter.

GETTING TO YOUR Z-SCORE

With a little practice, scoring prospects using the Push-button Zebra will become second nature. In fact, many prospects can be scored in about five minutes. In basic terms, when assessing a prospect, you simply enter a score from 0 to 4 for each attribute. The score you choose should reflect where on the worst-prospect-to-perfect-prospect continuum your prospect falls. You'll notice that the PBZ template has two columns on the right: date and comment. If you don't have enough information to score a prospect in one of the categories, select 0 as the score and enter an action step you need to take to get the information you need in the comment column. Also enter a date by which you need to gather the information. Once you've scored a prospect on each attribute, the spreadsheet will add up the scores for a total. This is your Z-score.

The spreadsheet contains comments attached to each of the cells. These comments allow for a complete, self-teaching description of how to score each attribute, making the PBZ a very personal and powerful tool. (Note: To view the comments, simply position your cursor over any cell with a red triangle in the corner.

To add your own comments or edit the comments already in the template, right-click on the cell and select "Edit comment" from the pop-up menu.)

Let's explore how a prospect can be analyzed based on the seven attributes to get to a Z-score. To illustrate the process, we'll use Kurt's PBZ.

Company

Let's look at the first attribute—company—in Kurt's PBZ and how he scored the current company he's evaluating, Transformers, Inc., a company Kurt thinks is a good opportunity for C3 and a good test case for his PBZ. Kurt scores Transformers as a 4 for the company characteristics, meaning they are a very good fit for the C3 solution, at least for the company attribute.

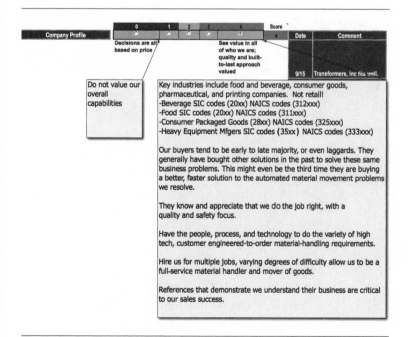

The Company Score

In Kurt's PBZ, if a particular prospect is price conscious to an extreme, the company score would be 0, the score given to a poor prospect fit for that attribute. Therefore, Transformers must not be very price conscious and likely is more focused on the value the solution has to offer, understanding that C3 will complete the job with a quality and safety focus. Kurt also knows that Transformers has a reputation for producing quality products themselves. This reputation translates into a desire to buy quality solutions, again providing further evidence they are worthy of a 4 in the company attribute.

Transformers is an electronic equipment manufacturer, and C3 does particularly well with electronics manufacturing companies (SIC code 36xx; 17 percent of C3 customers). Kurt and his team know that, on the product-adoption life cycle, C3 buyers tend to be early to late majority, or even laggard buyers. Their customers generally have bought other solutions in the past to solve the same business problems C3 addresses. This might even be the third time they are buying a better, faster solution to their automated material movement supply-chain problems. Kurt knows references that demonstrate an understanding of their business are critical to C3 sales success. Kurt believes that Transformers is a late majority buyer.

Operations

In the operations category, prospects who characteristically cherry-pick using C3 products and solutions are not desirable. This tendency would give the prospect an operations score of 0 or 1. In operational terms, an ideal prospect is one that sees the value of C3's customer-engineered solutions, and knows that is the best way to address their complex material-handling supply-chain needs. The more apparent these two characteristics become with a given prospect, the more desirable that prospect will be, which would result in a score of 3 or 4.

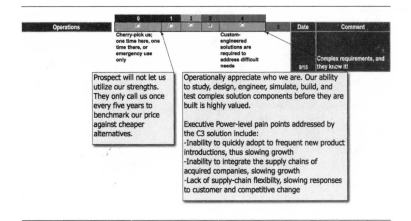

The Operations Score

Kurt has scored the operations characteristic for Transformers as a 3. Transformers knows it has complex requirements and that a simple out-of-the-box solution will not work for them. The engineer-to-order capabilities of C3 are recognized as a point of competitive differentiation and a capability it needs to ensure that the company receives the right solution for the material-handling side of their supply-chain requirements. Kurt has provided a lot of detail in this section (see the description in the figure) to ensure that his sales team stays where they bring real competitive advantage.

Access to Power

Perhaps the most important section of the Push-button Zebra is the access to Power score. If you can't get to a high score on this point, the prospect is not likely to be a Zebra. Take a minute and remember the last time you thought you were in a good position to get the business from a prospect, only to be outflanked by a competitor who had a relationship with the person making the buy decision. Painful experiences like these are great teachers of the consequences of not working with Power, and why this score is so important.

Without access to Power, your scores for all other attributes might be questionable, as might be your ability to ever get the business. Verifying your scores for all other attributes requires a meeting with Power (unless you have enough information to immediately rule out the prospect). Until Power confirms there is funding for the project or product, there is no funding. Until Power confirms that they care about the business issues or pain points your solution addresses, you have no solution. And finally, Power is the only one who can commit to buy your solution. Without access to Power you might be in for a very long sales cycle, or worse yet, a loss to "nondecision," where the prospect decides to spend its discretionary capital on something other than your solution. We'll delve into identifying Power's pain points and how to meet with Power in the next two chapters, but for now, at least understand that this score is critical to the success of your sales efforts.

A low Push-button Zebra score for access to Power should always be accompanied by a date and an action step in the comment field that indicates how you will work to get access to Power, or determine if it's possible.

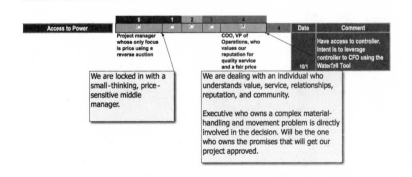

The Access to Power Score

For Kurt's PBZ, being forced to a project manager whose main concern is price is considered very undesirable. If the prospect continuously pushes the sales representative to lower-level project managers, the access to Power score would be a 0 or a 1. The closer the prospect gets to the ideal—the sales representative and C3 overall have access to the COO or VP of operations—the more desirable the prospect will be, and will score a 3 or a 4. Notice how Kurt specifically addressed, by title, who Power is and what his or her responsibilities are.

Kurt gave Transformers a score of 4 for access to Power. Transformers had allowed C3 access to the COO. The COO had authorized C3 to investigate how a highly engineered C3 solution could fulfill the company's complex requirements. Transformers valued the C3 approach, and Power had supported C3 efforts to design and propose the best possible solution for its requirements.

Funding

Funding, like access to Power, is an important attribute of Kurt's Zebra. Kurt has learned that understanding the finance process at a prospect is key to getting projects approved. If the process associated with funding isn't fully understood, this attribute is scored as a 0 or no higher than a 1.

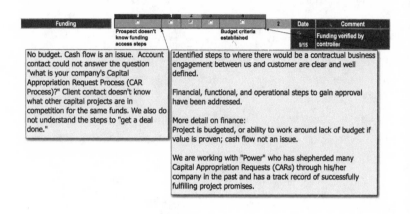

The Funding Score

Notice this C3 prospect is scored as a 2 in the funding attribute because funding has not yet been confirmed by Power at Transformers. A project that is budgeted or funded has no guarantee of actually happening. Companies have limited discretionary dollars. Competition for every dollar is evaluated against every other use for that same dollar. The projects that get approved are the ones with Power-level sponsorship and commitment. And even though the COO of Transformers is sponsoring C3 to create and prove the value of a supply-chain solution, there is still no guarantee that the project will ultimately go through. C3 has not yet received answers to its funding-related questions, so Kurt scored it a 2. Once C3 finishes its analysis and presents back to the COO (Power), this score will increase.

ROI

If your Zebras are primarily companies in the early majority, late majority, or even the laggards, successful sales will have to be based on value. Value quantified into an ROI will help distinguish you from your competition and against other projects competing for those same discretionary funding dollars. Overall, if you can't predict the value you'll be able to produce for a prospect, you really can't score that prospect higher than a 1 until you gather more information and develop a valid estimate of ROI.

In chapter 5, we will present a spectacular tool that will form the basis of your sales approach once you've begun the buying cycle with a prospect. It will help you determine the value you create in very specific terms, including ROI, payback period, and other important financial metrics. This analysis will be based on Power's pain points, which we'll discuss in chapter 4. For C3, a prospect where they have not been able to quantify the benefits would have a low ROI score of 0 or 1. The closer the prospect gets to the ideal—C3 has been able to quantify the value of the solution for this prospect and Power agrees with the ROI and that it is likely to be achieved—the more desirable this prospect will be, earning a score of 3 or even 4.

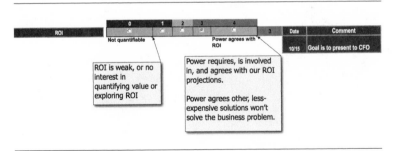

The ROI Score

Kurt has given Transformers a score of 1, because Power has not yet seen or agreed with C3's ROI projections. When the COO of Transformers confirms that the ROI applies to C3 only and not to competitors' offerings, C3 will be in a strong position and this score will go up. Remember, the PBZ is a living document, so your initial score for this attribute might be low, as is the case for Transformers. Once you meet with Power and present your prediction of the ROI, you'll be able to adjust your score as appropriate. And with these tools and techniques, you will meet Power!

Technology

In today's complex sales environment, knowing how your prospect feels about technology may determine whether you win or lose the deal. Technology discussions can be as emotionally charged as discussions about religion or politics. You can argue your point until you're blue in the face, but in the end, it's unlikely you are going to change somebody else's mind. You'll never "win" the argument. With technology, sometimes you just don't fit, and you may have lost before your buying cycle even begins. If your solution runs counter to the technology direction of a company, present to Power once, and if unsuccessful, you need to move on. For example, in software, if your solution runs on a Microsoft database and not on Oracle, you will run into companies that have Oracle-only technology standards. Your sales department may spend months solving business issues, doing demonstrations, creating proposals, and proving value, only to find out your solution is not technologically compatible with the stated direction of your prospect. You lost before you began!

Even simple solutions or products have technology advantages, which is why technology is a key component of your Zebra. For example, you might question how technology would play a role in helping to differentiate a car dealership. Even though a technology advantage is not as critical here as it might be in a complex sales cycle, it is still very important. And a car dealership might learn that prospects that do not recognize and value the technological advances of their vehicles, their service department, and their business do not buy from them.

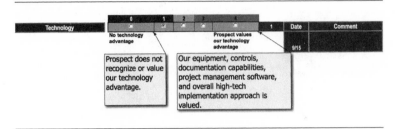

The Technology Score

Kurt's Push-button Zebra addresses the topic of technology rather generically, until you look at the detail comments. When the prospect doesn't acknowledge the technology advantage, they should receive a low score. When the prospect understands this competitive differentiation, the technology attribute is scored as a 3 or a 4.

Kurt scored Transformers as a 4. Transformers values C3's support of an open environment and its ability to engineer a solution tailored to Transformers' specific needs. And the C3 reputation for designing and building built-to-last solutions was a key reason the COO allowed C3 to be involved in a design-build process.

Service

Every company has a different approach to service, so it's important to understand what your customers value about your service offerings. Identifying a prospect's service needs will help you accurately score this attribute.

Like C3, a company we worked with did not have the service resources of its two main, larger competitors. And unlike those competitors, the company did not have strong relationships with the consulting firms who made a business of installing their solution. If they were going to win, their prospect had to have a strong desire to leverage the company's train-the-trainer approach. They would bring in highly trained experts for a very short period of time to train the client's internal experts and turn over responsibility for the subsequent implementation of the solution. Prospects that weren't open to this approach just weren't a good fit.

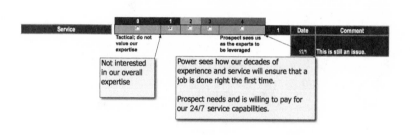

The Service Score

Service is a key point of differentiation for C3. The company is the only one that uses a train-the-trainer approach to implementation and service. When a prospect wants to become self-sufficient quickly, C3 offers a definite advantage, so these prospects would receive a fairly high score. If a prospect wanted the help of a consultant or constant hand-holding, C3 would not be able or willing to provide this level of service, and the prospect would score a 0 or 1.

Transformers has a reputation of negotiating down the cost of service. The attitude is that service is a cost that should decrease every year. Pressure to get the suppliers to deliver more for less each year is a key part of the company's market reputation. For this reason, Kurt scored Transformers' service score as a 1. The only reason Kurt scored it a 1 and not a 0 is because Transformers does value the talent C3 has to service the project and, at least initially, seems willing to pay for that service. Kurt is hopeful that Transformers will see that the C3 service philosophy of teaching them to fish, as opposed to giving them a fish, will ultimately allow them to achieve the most value at the least cost. Over time, once Power agrees this service strategy is best, this score will go up.

WHAT TO DO WITH A Z-SCORE

You've done it! You've analyzed a prospect based on your best- and worst-case sales scenarios, and you've come up with a quantifiable result. Isn't that amazing? You may not be as excited as we are—yet. But that's because you probably don't know exactly what your number means or how to proceed from here. Take a look at the bottom of the PBZ spreadsheet. We've inserted a note about point ranges and what they mean.

 WAKE-UP CALL

- If the Z-score for a prospect is 0 to 9, that prospect is a high risk and probably isn't a good fit for your company.

- If the Z-score for a prospect is 10 to 19, the prospect presents some risk and may or may not be worth pursuing.

- If the Z-score is 20 to 28, the prospect is likely a Zebra, so chase after it!

Let's look at each of these point ranges and develop a plan for how to proceed. A low-scoring prospect may tempt you to remove them from your list. If this is your first pass through the Push-button Zebra and the resulting score is low only because you don't have sufficient information, continue to pursue the opportunity until you have enough information to reach a valid score. If this prospect is a key account and is in one of your preferred verticals, meet with Power before you remove the opportunity from your pipeline. Meet with Power early, before wasting valuable resources. Once you feel like you've reached a final score, if the prospect is still at less than ten or is on the lower end of the "some risk" category, you should seriously consider removing it from your pipeline.

If a prospect has a mid-range score, indicating that there might be some risk in pursuing the opportunity, you should assess where you are strong and where you are weak and develop a strategy to improve upon your weaknesses. If you are not at the right executive level in the deal, you might decide to invest enough time to get to Power. If you are still in the lower end of the "some risk" category after meeting with Power, you should consider exiting the deal.

And of course, if a prospect scores high, as a Zebra, pursue, pursue, pursue! Don't stop unless or until you discover any information that would make you lower the score.

Kurt's Z-score for Transformers is an 18, which puts them on the higher end of the "some risk" category. Kurt should immediately zero in on those attribute scores that are particularly low and strategize a possible solution with his team. Kurt can see where C3 is strong and where there are challenges. He therefore knows the best sales talent to leverage to improve his chance of success. Kurt has a potential Zebra worth additional sales resources and will continue to pursue this opportunity. At this point in the process, Transformers is the Zebra Kurt and his team want to hunt!

Once you have finished your Push-button Zebra, test your Zebra with your best customers. What is the average score? Then score the five deals you most recently won. What Zebra score did it take to win? Next, score the companies that bought from your competitors. How do they compare? This process will help you prove or improve the accuracy of your Zebra profile and your Push-button Zebra and provide you with additional insights and ideas about your Zebra. Finally, score your entire sales forecast pipeline. What is your average score? Based on your Zebra scores, which deals in your pipeline should be removed?

When you implement this system, you can use it to assess your forecast each quarter. Take special note of the Zebra scores at the beginning of each quarter. What Zebra score at the beginning of the quarter translates into a 90 percent close rate by the end of the quarter? One customer of ours definitively knows that a Zebra score of 23 at the beginning of the quarter translates into revenue at the end of the quarter 91 percent of the time! Once you can answer this question for yourself, you will be able to accurately predict your quarterly revenue. Additionally, accurate knowledge of a weak quarter at the beginning of the quarter can help create urgency and action to more quickly alleviate sales problems.

We hope you are as excited about the Push-button Zebra as we are. It is a great tool that can drastically improve how you spend your time and resources. But it may be difficult to get buy-in for this new approach at all levels of your organization. This is a problem Kent is facing, even though his team's sales numbers have been high.

Kent quickly ends the call he is on when his assistant informs him that Scotty is on the phone.

"Kent, I have some good news for you. Bill Kaneely called me with a lead for you."

Great, Kent thinks, rolling his eyes. Bill Kaneely is the board member who was looking for Kurt's job just two weeks ago. Keeping his response professional, Kent says pleasantly, "Oh, good. Who has the details?"

"I do. Listen up: Cheftime Foods is looking for a new solution. Bill has a relationship with a key player there and has gotten C3 on the vendor list. Bill's relationship will go a long way in this account. This is a golden opportunity for you, Kent. Don't screw it up."

What a miserable "golden opportunity!" Kent received an RFP for Cheftime Foods just last week. Yesterday, when he reviewed his pipeline against his Push-button Zebra, Cheftime was one of the deals he eliminated. Cheftime runs its business too much like a previous C3 customer that was not a good fit. Support of this unhappy customer had cost lots of additional sales time, and now they were refusing to pay. Worse yet, they would never be a reference for C3.

Kent had run Cheftime through his Push-button Zebra and they scored a nine, making them a high-risk prospect. Cheftime was far from a Zebra. Just a week or so after Scotty's directive to drive more sales activity, and Kent feels his resolve being tested.

"Scotty, I already have the RFP from Cheftime, and I've determined that we are not a good fit." Kent explains how his team has jump-started sales, describing they strategically identify the type of deals where he knows C3 fits best. "The outcome of this process," Kent says, "is the Push-button Zebra. The PBZ is designed to identify the deals that will provide C3 and me with the best opportunities for success." He further explains how he has stack-ranked his current prospects to prioritize his time and how this process helps him set a strategy that accentuates C3's strengths and addresses C3's weaknesses with a given prospect.

Kent pauses, then decides to go for broke: "Scotty, sometimes C3 as an organization seems to feel good about pursuing a high-proposal-dollar activity simply because it represents effort, not realizing we are effectively diluting our resources. And opportunities that should have been won are put at risk because they don't receive the appropriate focus. This is the thinking behind the Zebra philosophy that I live by," Kent concludes, starting to perspire as he awaits a response.

After a long silence, Scotty begins, "Kent, what you just said makes intuitive sense to me."

"It does? . . . I mean, yes. I think so, too."

"But," Scotty continues, "you still need to pursue Cheftime. Bill Kaneely's friend personally requested that you respond to the RFP and participate in the sales cycle. He told his boss that C3 is one of the best in the industry. When you called to say C3 wouldn't be responding to the RFP, he got on the phone immediately with Bill. All of this happened just this morning."

"Scotty, I've reviewed this opportunity in detail," Kent protests, holding his ground. "I involved a sales engineer who had already reviewed the RFP and further resource requests. Drawing on input from my salespeople and sales engineers, I have determined that I would invest four man-days in the RFP response, three man-days in other preparation, and another three man-days in actual sales cycle execution. That's ten man-days of my time on an opportunity that I should not win, based on where our solution fits. Even if I did win, we would probably run into an implementation problem."

"You present a powerful argument," Scotty concedes. "What if Bill's contact was willing to pay for our time? Many of our prospects do paid studies these days. I bet Bill Kaneely can get him to do it. What do we charge for services now—$100 to $200 per hour?"

"I have new thinking when it comes to paid studies," Kent replies. "I pursue only Zebras, even if a client is willing to pay, because my real cost is the *opportunity cost* of not using my time and our best people where we have the best opportunity to win."

"Kent, Kent, Kent . . ." Scotty sighs. "You're not making this easy. I have stayed patient so far. What are you talking about, 'opportunity costs'?"

"Scotty, I have a very large sales quota that I have to achieve."

"Yes, you do."

"If we divide my quota by the 220 business days in a year, we find that I need to generate many thousands of dollars of sales of C3 products and services per day to meet that quota. So the opportunity costs are thousands of dollars per day for me and our presales people, not the couple hundred dollars per hour we would bill for the services. I need to work on—we need to work on—opportunities that have the potential to generate thousands of dollars per day to be successful. So you see, if Bill's friend pays us to work on a non-Zebra opportunity, he would be shortchanging me and you by thousands."

At this point Kent can tell that Scotty is not his normal combative self, but even his abnormal patience is starting to wear thin. "Kent, politics are involved here, and Bill Kaneely has committed you to participate."

"Less than two weeks ago you told Kurt he had ninety days—now only about eighty days—to get significantly more business . . . Kurt's my friend, but I don't want to end up like him. You need to defend my path, Scotty. I am on the right path; I can feel it, and the numbers support it. And I think you can see that."

Again Scotty lets the line go silent. Finally, he offers, "I'll take care of Kaneely . . . You go drive some revenue." Scotty hangs up the telephone without saying good-bye.

As Kent thinks through how he explained the process and why it works to Scotty, he feels strong, and he realizes he may have just overcome his biggest hurdle.

The main thrust of the Zebra philosophy isn't about walking away, although that is a possibility. All opportunities are reviewed against the profile before you pursue a prospect and before every major step in the Zebra Buying Cycle. From there you make a decision to engage or to stay engaged. This way your eyes are open to all the possible strengths and weaknesses that determine your chances for mutual success with a prospect. The idea is to evaluate each opportunity before you use, or continue to use, any sales resources to pursue it.

The Zebra way is a quantifiable niche strategy that works very effectively when followed. Although an easy-to-understand concept, it requires discipline in execution if you are to receive its rewards. The Push-button Zebra makes execution of the Zebra process much easier and helps ensure that, as a rule, no high-potential resources are wasted on low-potential opportunities.

CHAPTER 4

DEFINE POWER'S PAIN POINTS

FOR MOST OF YOUR SALES CAREER, you've probably believed that the success of your product or solution is tied to how well it addresses the operational needs of your customer, right? If you sell software, you are successful at selling it because the people who use it like the three-way financial matching capability or finite scheduling or solid model three-dimensional views or other features and functions that drive the value associated with using it. If you sell earth-moving equipment, you probably think you've been successful because of the payload capacity of your equipment, the 960-horsepower diesel power plant, or the plush, air-conditioned cabin. You can always make a sale by emphasizing features and functions, right? Guess what? You're wrong! That's not why they bought.

Features and functions *are* important to middle managers, and most companies sell to these managers. But this usually results in a continuous selling-and-reselling process where you sell to the middle managers, and they sponsor you in to the executive or, worse, they become the ones who try to sell your solution to their boss, boss's boss, or boss's boss's boss. This is one of the primary reasons why sales cycles are so long and unpredictable. The better way we have been describing requires that you start and stay with Power. To do that, you have to determine the executive-level pain points your solution can address.

 WAKE-UP CALL

As we've been saying for the past few chapters, if you want to sell more and sell faster, you need to work with Power, the person who will make the ultimate decision to buy. And if you want to sell to Power, you need to think like Power thinks, which is often far removed from features and functions. Power is concerned about higher-level business issues, and you have to address these specific pain points if Power is to see any value in what you're selling. The Zebra way of selling is valid only when you identify the existence of these pain points within your prospective accounts.

Here are some sample pain points that may be relevant to your clients:

- competitive advantage and innovation
- increase profit
- increase the value of their brand (hard to measure, but extremely valuable when accomplished)

- ability to address customer-initiated change (for example, two-day delivery of custom product that used to take two weeks)
- increase customer loyalty (can be measured by repeat business)
- ability to address industry-initiated change (for example, Internet business-to-business-based connection to your suppliers, improving accuracy and reducing cost and the cycle time it takes to get deliveries to customers)
- better use of existing assets (for example, increase facility utilization from eight or sixteen hours per day to twenty-four hours a day, seven days a week)
- ability to respond to, rather than react to, competitive pressure, and perhaps even leapfrog the competition
- improve efficiency and overall efficacy
- exceed industry growth
- improve compliance or reduce risk
- improve visibility and control
- for public companies, improve the stock price and thus the market capitalization (stock price times number of outstanding shares of stock)

I'll bet most of these issues seem less complex to you than the operational issues or the features and functions you like to discuss with customers. Power's pain points, by definition, are at a higher level and easier to talk about in the abstract, but they generally are not easy to accomplish or to prove that you can accomplish. How does your solution help your customers address issues like those we listed above? If you can't answer that question, you can't prove your value to Power.

The entire Zebra process builds on this point. Identifying Power's pain points is the first step in understanding how to sell to Power within Zebra prospects, and thus the key to the success of the Zebra methodology. Focusing on these issues changes each step of the sales cycle or buying cycle. As a sales organization, you should not consider the sales process to be truly finished until a customer achieves the value you promised, the value that is tied to addressing the pain points. Therefore, you must

- Know from the outset what the pain points are.
- Ensure that your proposal is aligned to address the pain points.
- Ensure that you constantly measure and report your progress toward those goals to Power.
- Know that you aren't done until you help Power achieve the promises that led to the authorization of the project and the purchase of the product.

POWER'S PAIN POINTS ARE DIFFERENT

Take a moment to consider the selling points you've relied on in the past. They probably relate to the functionality of your product, the special features, the key differentiators compared to competitors' products. In short, they are probably operational selling points. And you may believe that to move beyond those basic selling techniques, you simply have to show that your product or service offers a positive or even substantial ROI. With that, you'll have what you need to sell at the executive level—because executives are concerned only with what the numbers tell them. Wrong! Today, a positive ROI is not enough. Power likely has a number of projects with positive ROIs but doesn't have the budget to approve all of them. You have to prove that your project or product can address problems that Power is responsible for solving. You probably will have to use numbers to support those claims, but the numbers have to be tied to specific business issues.

While on the phone with Mark Nem, Kurt is realizing that ROI is not enough. He called Mark to ask for a second chance—a chance to present a revised solution that better meets Nem's needs. After creating the Push-button Zebra, Kurt ran Nem's through it and discovered that they were a 25, and that he could confidently score them as a 4 for access to Power. *I'm going directly to Power*, he thought, realizing how critical it was to salvage the account. He had made some initial contacts the previous week, before the Zebra creation, but he didn't try to get Mark Nem on the phone until today.

"Mark, Scotty shared your input with me, and I appreciate your position. I know we need to find a better solution for you and make sure that the solution is successful in every way."

"Listen, Kurt. We have about twenty new projects under evaluation here. About half of them will pass technical, functional, and investment hurdles. But we're going to fund only two or three over the next two years. And just because we put out the RFP for this project doesn't mean that the project will definitely get approved. If that's going to happen, and happen with you, you've got to show me something special. What you submitted was fine, but it wasn't going to be able to compete with other projects. It had a positive ROI, it met management's specs, but we are considering other, unrelated projects that will help us grow in the future. I don't see value in yours like I see in these other projects. And given the recent problems we've had with your team from a follow-through perspective, I couldn't see how to continue our relationship."

Kurt decides to take a chance. "I know we didn't present the best solution for you, Mark. We knew once the consultant got involved with this RFP that we were in trouble. He's favorably disposed to our largest competitor, and the RFP that was created favored their solution. We grumbled about the unfair playing field and the consultant's obvious bias, but what did we do to change the situation? Nothing. And that hurt you as well as us. To be honest, we don't believe that this RFP accurately represents your needs, and we didn't do a good job of explaining that. We've done some research on Nem's and found in your annual report that improved efficiency and customer retention are key business issues for Nem's. Can you give us another shot? We'd like to address these issues. We want to create a proposal that wows you—that solves problems we know you have that you haven't even told us about."

"Well, that would be great, Kurt, but I don't know if I believe it's possible." Mark pauses for a few moments. "Okay, Kurt. You've piqued my interest. You've got your second chance. You'd better make it worth it."

Kurt hangs up the phone feeling elated. Then reality sinks in. "Great," he mutters. "What do we do now?" He stares at his desk for a moment, trying to avoid the call he knows he has to make. Finally, he picks up the phone and dials. "Kent, I hate to keep bothering you, but I need some help—again."

Before you can successfully sell to Power, you need to understand how Power's pain points are different from those of lower-level managers and end users. This is particularly important because RFPs—those tools that are probably driving your current sales cycles—are typically focused on operational- and user-level business issues. Consequently, most sales teams understand the operations-level business issues and user-level business issues of their prospects and customers. But if you don't have a handle on Power's pain points, you can't accurately identify your Zebras, your accounts won't be forecast-worthy, and you can't create proposals that will force the success of your solution. In the end, you'll need to understand what the issues are at all levels to make your product truly successful for the customer. The table shown below presents some examples taken directly from a few companies' annual reports.

Power, Operations, and User Pain Points

Power's Pain Points	Operations' Pain Points	User's Pain Points
Leverage core assets of knowledge and technology to create shareholder value Drive rapid and dramatic growth Execute with precision Build commitment to delivering customer-relevant solutions Leverage cutting-edge technology, unique data, and advanced scoring analytics to provide total solutions for client needs Employ state-of-the-art e-marketing initiatives and Internet strategies that allow us to take advantage of the full potential of the Internet	Reduce labor Reduce inventory Increase throughput Increase inventory turns Reduce damage and scrap (These are the issues that fill most RFPs, so you should know them well.)	Simplify a job Increase ability to respond to customer requests Easily change setups, packaging, etc. (We won't go on here, as you probably know these issues well.)

Of course, it's not all contrast when it comes to operations' pain points versus Power's pain points. There is a strong, direct correlation between the two sets of issues: operational issues must be solved in order to achieve the bigger-picture goals. However, the simple fact of the matter is that in order to sell your solution at the level where the decisions truly happen, the Power level, you have to tie the issues that your solution solves into the issues that Power addresses. Your solution may well solve a large variety of operational issues that will help address Power's pain points, but until you make the leap and connect your solution specifically to the issues Power really cares about, you don't have a message that Power will be interested in hearing. In fact, when you talk operations-level issues with Power, she generally has to relegate you down in her organization because she doesn't even know the details behind the operational issues.

So how do you move beyond features and functions and basic financial stats? How do you determine Power's pain points? It's not hard, but it takes some legwork and some knowledge.

 ## WAKE-UP CALL

To identify Power's pain points, you have to

- Identify the Zebras in your customer base using your Zebra profile and Push-button Zebra (using preliminary scores).

- Interview customers' executives about why they bought from you (be sure to identify Power as part of this process, if you don't already know who Power is).

- Gather the key executive-level pain points they identified for purchasing your solution.

- Research your prospect (as Kurt researched Nem's) to determine if Power's pain points are similar to the pain points your solution typically addresses for your Zebras.

EXPLORE YOUR ZEBRA'S PAIN POINTS

When you developed your Zebra profile, you identified a host of characteristics that are common among your best customers, and therefore your best prospects. Now dig even deeper to find similar patterns in the real reasons your customers have bought from you in the past. Keep in mind that your customers bought because you solved Power's executive-level pain points, even if you didn't know what those pain points were at the time.

This process is something you'll have to do only once (like your Zebra profile), and then you'll need to just update the information you gather if the pain points of your customer base or new customers seem to be changing, or if you revamp your solution. The first step is to identify all Zebras in your customer base. Use your Push-button Zebra to score them. You will use those customers with preliminary Zebra scores of 22 or higher to form the basis of your research.

Review Project Documentation

The best way to uncover your customers' pain points is to go to your newly found Zebras and ask to see the internal documentation they used to get the project or deal approved. This documentation will give you valuable insight as to why approval to spend money on your solution, versus your competition's solution or other potential projects, was granted.

 WAKE-UP CALL

There is no better way to find the real decision maker (Power), the executive-level reasons your customers bought, and the project's internal financial goals than to scour the capital appropriation process.

Simple projects require simple justification. For complex projects, most companies use what's called a capital appropriation request, or CAR. Companies use CARs to evaluate alternative uses of a company's available capital. Every dollar of capital a company spends is evaluated against all other possible uses of that same dollar. The CAR usually includes financial calculations—ROI, net present value, economic value added, internal rate of return, payback period—to help make the comparison. Those financial goals will help you understand how your customers tie their promises to specific metrics.

Take a look at the box on page 97, "Finance for Salespeople 101." If those terms seem a little confusing, take the time now to research them until you have a strong understanding of them and feel comfortable that you could use them to communicate with prospects. (More education is available on our website at www.sellingtozebras.com in the Zebra University section. Download the "Building credibility with a CXO" presentation and, to really test your knowledge, download and take the financial terms quiz.) This is the financial language of Power! Keep in mind that after all the financial analysis is over, the projects that get approved are still those that solve Power's pain points. The more closely your solution is tied to these pain points, the more compelling your project proposal will be to your prospective buyer.

Finance for Salespeople 101

RETURN ON INVESTMENT: The number of times a project pays for itself over its lifetime. A 582 percent ROI over five years indicates that the project pays for itself almost six times (5.82 times, to be exact) over the five-year useful life of the project.

NET PRESENT VALUE: The stream of expected cash converted into value in terms of today's dollars. An NPV of $2.8 million means that the stream of expected benefit worth $3.7 million over a five-year period is worth $2.8 million when converted into today's dollars (using a discount rate of 10 percent). In other words, $3.7 million of value spread out over five years is the equivalent of $2.8 million today. Choosing an appropriate discount rate is crucial to the believability of the NPV calculation. A good practice of choosing the discount rate is to decide the rate that the capital needed for the project could return if invested in an alternative venture. If, for example, the capital required for a project can earn 10 percent elsewhere, use this discount rate in the NPV calculation to allow a direct comparison to be made between your project and the alternative.

ECONOMIC VALUE ADDED: The dollar amount of benefit created over the life of the project after removing all costs. These include the cost of the client's personnel to install and run a solution as well as the cost of capital used to purchase the solution. Because EVA considers the latter, some think EVA is the truest benefit calculation. A $2.3 million, five-year EVA indicates the project will return $2.3 million over five years, considering all costs, including that of the capital used to purchase the solution (in this example, we use 10 percent as the cost of capital). Even if money is not borrowed, financers will estimate a cost of capital based on what they could make investing the same dollars in the bank, in other low-risk options, or elsewhere in the business.

INTERNAL RATE OF RETURN: The interest rate you expect to make on your investment in a capital project. An example of IRR is the interest rate a bank pays for the use of your money. A five-year, 185 percent IRR means the project will generate a 185 percent return over five years.

PAYBACK PERIOD: The exact number of months it takes to get all the money back that will be invested in the project. A payback period of eight months, for example, means that a buyer will get his investment back eight months after writing you a check. The longer it takes to get the money back, the greater the risk that the project will never pay for itself or have a positive overall return.

Reviewing the CAR documentation will help you uncover three valuable pieces of information you can use to continue the development of your Zebra profile.

- Who is Power within your customer base (if you aren't sure yet)?
- What promises did Power make that got the project approved?
- What are the value-based goals of the project?

You may have already identified who Power is in the Zebras you've found in your customer base. If not, this process will be enlightening. For the rest of this chapter, we'll focus on the promises Power made to get the project approved, as those will reveal the pain points your solution addressed. In chapter 5, we'll explore the third piece of information: value.

Conduct Interviews

Although CAR documentation can be very revealing, some companies may not have such documentation. And even in companies that do have documentation, interviews with Power can reveal more information than you might find in written form. Therefore, once you've identified Power, you should do your best to set up an interview to ask specific questions about why she decided to buy your product over others.

Once you've gathered as much information as possible from your existing customers, turn to your recent losses to find out why they didn't choose your solution. You may already know this from your initial work on your Zebra profile, but can you identify the pain points your products didn't solve for those companies? Inevitably, that's why you lost that business. Our Kurt will offer some insights into these conversations.

The past week has been a big one for Kurt. A week ago, he believed he knew why his customers buy from him—what problems his products solve. As his team prepared their Zebra profile and Push-button Zebra, they discovered a lot about their customers and their product. But Kent told him that he needed to go further: he needed to identify the pain points the C3 solution solved in the customer base and determine how those pain points match up with what's happening at accounts like Nem's.

Kurt reviewed the materials his team had gathered from their best customers and discovered that they had previously only identified operational issues. And they had only rarely identified Power. Based on his conversation with Kent, he knew this wouldn't help him reach Mark Nem. He needed more feedback, and fast, so he sent his team out on an information hunt to their best customers.

Kurt's list of customers was selected based on Zebra fit. In addition to the Zebra fit, the key qualification for input in the project was that a Zebra team member had to convince the rest of the team that he or she had actually found Power. This task proved to be very valuable not only for the information it yielded but also for the contacts Kurt's people were able to make at levels in client companies that they had never before breached.

His team expected to discover that companies purchase C3 solutions to address operational issues like increasing product throughput and accuracy, reducing inventory and increasing inventory turns, reducing product damage, reducing labor expense, and so on. What they found surprises them.

The team learned, interestingly, that many multimillion-dollar projects had been won and installed without anyone from C3 ever meeting with Power. The team also concluded that the lack of access to Power was the primary reason for long sales cycles and lower-margin business, two key issues Kurt's Zebra team has been trying to address.

The process used to establish contact with Power was simple but bold. The team first established the reasons (sometimes conjectural) the client bought. They then hypothesized the quantifiable business benefit the client should have enjoyed based on the team's knowledge of the account. This approach created some interesting discussions with executives in the customer base.

Not one executive said they bought to increase inventory turns, though often inventory turns greatly improved. No one said they bought to reduce labor expense, yet labor expense was reduced.

Tom Dryden, COO of Tandim Manufacturing, purchased a C3 solution to support a lean manufacturing initiative designed to accelerate the growth of the company. This was Tom's—that is, Power's—pain point. This pain point translated into several related operational pain points: Tom's company could not compete with the Chinese on price. Tandim's differentiation had to be quicker delivery of frequently changing technology. As a result of the C3 solution, did Tandim enjoy lower labor costs? Yes. But it bought because of a broader and more politically connected overall strategy than had ever previously been imagined. Operationally, the C3 solution allowed it to deliver, in a matter of weeks, the same technology changes that the Chinese took months to deliver. As product life cycles shortened, this advantage was huge for Tandim Manufacturing—it solved Power's pain point of accelerating Tandim's growth! Tandim was not an isolated example. There were others who expressed the same growth desires.

Kurt's team also learned that customers bought to leverage C3's updated technology, unique data, and advanced scoring analytics, which helped to provide total solutions for their client needs. They specifically bought because C3 solutions bent, but didn't break, their present supply-chain paradigm. C3 seamlessly integrated and continued to help leverage their existing technology. Without a simple-to-use, easily adopted, seamlessly integrated solution, C3 would not have won the business, because they would have not delivered a solution that addressed Power's pain point of leveraging updated technology while still using their existing technology.

Kurt's customers were looking for a solution to support changes that their market, in many cases, forced on them. They did not want to debug or fix a solution; they expected the C3 product to work properly and to integrate with their existing technology base and overall strategy. They wanted evolution, not revolution.

Next, Kurt's team reached out to their noncustomers. One opportunity lost last year, Tech Dyna, bought a solution they were convinced would provide more competitive advantage than the C3 solution. When Kurt's team had evaluated the loss, all agreed that C3 didn't fit well with Tech Dyna, but no one could explain why. After talking with the vice president of logistics at Tech Dyna they learned that the decision swung in favor of the competition because Tech Dyna wanted to blaze a new market and the competitor offered a way to leapfrog Tech Dyna's competition. The company bought a vision of the future that was sold by C3's competition. That is why it was willing to take the higher risk the competitor represented. Although C3 was perceived as being safe, it was also closer to the status quo.

Now Kurt sits with his team in the conference room, brainstorming. It's clear that the division's best customers and prospects bought C3's solutions because they work. C3's customers wanted the solution because it had also benefited other companies they knew and trusted. The team concludes that one or more of the following issues is confirmed by Power as an "eminent event" critical to the ongoing success of the business.

C3 customer pain points:

- Global markets and global competition are driving change and they have to catch up.
- Cost cutting is important, but executives are looking to grow their business, and supply-chain integration is seen as a vehicle to address speed-to-market issues that would help to grow their business.
- Proliferation of products is causing design and manufacturing slowdown.
- The current processes were designed fifteen or more years ago and no longer fit business requirements, and therefore need refreshing.
- Acquisitions are driving growth; integration of acquisitions is slowing that growth.

C3 prospects want tried-and-true solutions that are stable and will be easily integrated to avoid costly, time-consuming changeover. Those prospects that are looking for leading edge, or bleeding edge, will most often buy from the competition.

The team also discusses the fact that most of the contact within their customer base has been with middle managers and project managers, not true Power. As they discover the reasons Power has approved the purchase of a C3 solution, they discover how to grow their business by identifying opportunities before prospects send RFPs or RFIs. This discovery is going to help Kurt's team uncover more opportunities in the marketplace.

But Kurt is currently focused on one opportunity: Nem's. He believes that he is ready to establish the needs that the C3 solution can address for Nem's in a way that Mark Nem will appreciate.

RESEARCH YOUR PROSPECT

Once you have asked Power in your existing customers the pain points your solution was purchased to solve, you can research these issues within your prospect. It's best to gather all of your information in one document for easy reference. To access a template that shows you what this document might look like, go to the Zebra University at www.sellingtozebras.com and download the document called Research Template.

To begin your search for evidence to confirm that your prospect does in fact have some of the business issues that you solve, start by reading the letter from the CEO or chairman in your prospect's annual report. The annual report for a public company can almost always be found right on its website. The report will discuss the most important initiatives and challenges presently facing the company.

You're going to use this research to penetrate your prospect account, so when describing the pain points that you can address for your prospect, it's important that you use the exact words used in the annual report to describe these issues. You want to communicate using Power's language. A good way to do this is to cut and paste key terms and phrases right from the chairman's or CEO's letter into your research document. By using the words from a prospect's annual report and tying them directly to the business issues that your product can help address, you have begun the process of creating a compelling case to penetrate your Zebra at the level of Power.

If your prospect is not a public company, there are other ways to gather the pain-point information so important to Power-level penetration. Try these proven techniques:

- Look at any news, current events, or press release links (if available) on the company website for any recent articles regarding major initiatives, business issues, mergers, growth, loss, etc.
- Look at the "Careers" (or similar) section of the company's website for any information about their hiring practices, current openings, information regarding culture, etc.
- The following Internet searches (particularly using Google) will help you find the pain-point information you covet:
    - Company name and "goals"
    - Company name and "financials"
    - Company name and the specific area you address (Kurt would enter the company name and "supply chain")
    - Company name and "product launch"
    - Company name and "employee" (may give you articles on human resources initiatives, such as training events)
    - Company name and "technology" (this search will sometimes produce information about current technology partners, vendors, or initiatives)
    - Company name and "solutions" (this search will sometimes produce information about how they position themselves in their market)
    - Company name and "growth"

- Company name and any other key word to describe the information you are searching for to create any number of searches. Often you will come up with new key words to use, so always look for other possibilities while searching.

- Executive names (Searching by executives' names, especially the CEO, CFO, or various VPs, will often lead to articles in which they are quoted—articles regarding initiatives, growth, etc. You can also find biographies this way. Forbes. com offers profiles of many executives of larger and smaller companies.)

- Bizjournals.com (American City Business Journals Inc. publishes in many of the major metropolitan areas. You can search the archives and then be set up as a free user of their site.)

Once you've identified Power's pain points in your prospect, what do you do with that information? Well, one of two things will happen: the pain points will align with the pain points your solution addresses, or they won't. If they do, then you have more proof that you're working with a Zebra. This type of proof is particularly important if the original Zebra score was borderline. This information might not directly improve that score, but it might give you more insight into some of the characteristics of your prospect that will improve the score. Regardless, even if the score is borderline, if you think Power's needs align with your strengths, then you need to keep pursuing the prospect.

Now, if you are unable to find proof that Power's pain points align with the pain points you've identified in your customer base, assuming they are otherwise a Zebra with a healthy Z-score, continue your research. But you'll be amazed how many times you'll find the right nuggets of information in the company's annual report. Why are we so confident you'll find issues you address? Because there just are not that many Power-level business issues. There are lots of ways to solve them. But the executive-level issues list is a finite set: growth, leveraging technology or other strengths, improving competitive advantage, etc. "Then why don't more people sell this way?" you ask. Because they didn't know it was this easy!

Kurt needs to deliver something spectacular to Mark Nem, something that will wow him and prove that C3 is the company Nem's should be working with. He's excited about the list of pain points his team has created, so he dives in to the research on Nem's business issues to see how they connect.

Kurt turns to the annual reports for the last two years. In the letter from Mark Nem himself, Kurt finds some promising information. The letter is peppered with phrases such as "growth through acquisition" and "strong desire to expand business with existing customers to spur growth." Combining this information with the two pain points he already discussed with Mark on the phone (improved efficiency and customer retention), Kurt knows he's on the right path. He then does some media searches and finds an article in the local business paper that addresses recent improvements in the company's financial results. Finally, Kurt pulls the information together and creates a list of what he believes Mark Nem's pain points to be.

- Commitment to delivering customer-relevant innovations
- Interested in more rapid development of customer-relevant solutions

- Proud of the speed and tenacity with which associates created and adopted the changes necessary to serve ever-evolving customer needs, but wants more faster
- Committed to creating a strong foundation to achieve future growth
- Pleased with improvements made, yet far from satisfied; has a mind-set that every day brings a new opportunity for improvement
- Continuing to deploy a capability called Rapid Continuous Improvement (RCI), a structured set of tools and processes that enable waste elimination while making improvements in safety, quality, delivery, and cost

Kurt now knows that a C3 supply chain would generate tremendous value for Nem's, based on the way his solution would directly tie in to Nem's ongoing initiatives. Mark Nem himself publicly stated that Nem's was focused on customer-relevant solutions delivered with speed and tenacity to spur growth. A C3 supply-chain solution that helped reduce the time to market and delivery of Nem's products would certainly be a customer-relevant solution. And the RCI initiative could be further enhanced with C3 tools and processes that would help them stay on their desired path.

Now he's ready to take the next step. He feels confident that he has identified the right issues and that he's ready to meet with Mark Nem.

Understanding how your solution can help your prospects address their most important business challenges and opportunities is the crux of the Zebra sales model. When you do this, you can sell to Power, and if you can sell to Power, you will be able to overcome your own pain points: low margins, long sales cycles, and increased competition.

CHAPTER 5

PREDICT THE VALUE OF YOUR SOLUTION

WHAT HAVE WE BEEN WORKING TOWARD so far in this book? What is it we need in order to improve our sales, to reduce cycle time, to improve margins, and to address our other sales-related pain points? We need to be able to sell to Power in our Zebra prospects. We've made some good headway in that direction, but there's a last piece of the puzzle that's missing. And it's a pretty critical piece.

To sell to Power, we have to be able to convince Power that we have a solution that will address her pain points. The pain points, as we've said, are the only things that will drive Power to spend money. So, identifying those pain points is critical, but proving that we can create a valuable solution to address them, one that has been successfully implemented in other companies, is also necessary. Otherwise, why would Power buy from you?

WAKE-UP CALL

Most businesses today can articulate their value proposition, or the overall value they believe they have created for their existing customers. But you have to ask yourself: How does that value tie to the specific business issues our customers have told us are important to them? Without an answer to that question, you're dead in the water with Power. So, we are going to help you get in front of prospects and confidently say: "Based on the value we've created by solving specific business issues for customers of similar size, in similar industries, we predict we will also be able to create this value for you." And that, you will find, is a very powerful statement. But you're going to have to back it up with real data.

The process for developing the data and tools you'll need to make this statement to Power and support it is straightforward:

- Conduct audits of the customer base to uncover the quantifiable value your solution has produced by solving the executive-level pain points.

- Gather specific data about your prospect (if you haven't already).

- Use your research and your knowledge of the value your solution has created in the past to predict the value you can create for the prospect.

Kurt is examining the information he has pulled together for Mark Nem on Nem's business issues when his phone rings.

"Hey, Kurt, it's Kent."

"Hey, Kent. Wow, you're calling me for once! How are you?"

"Good, good. I was just calling to check in. I haven't heard from you for a few days, and I was becoming rather attached to our almost daily chats."

"Now you're just mocking me. I haven't called because things are going really well. I'm preparing for a meeting with Mark Nem next week. I figured out his pain points and I'm ready to meet with him."

"Wow, that's fast! You've already gathered the data on how your products will generate value for him?"

"What do you mean?"

"Well, if you're going to meet with him and talk to him about his pain points, don't you think that as you describe how the C3 solution will help him address those issues you should also communicate what value you'll generate where and how?"

"Yes," Kurt sighs. "I suppose I should. I don't imagine you have any ideas about how to do that, oh sales guru."

"As a matter of fact ..."

UNCOVERING THE VALUE YOU CREATE

If you've been working through the process, you should have a research document for your prospect that outlines the business issues your product can help them address. Now you need to answer the question: What value has been generated for my existing customers by addressing their executive-level pain points? You'll be able to take the answer to this question and extrapolate from it to answer the same question for your prospect.

How do you get to this powerful place? One of the easiest ways to assess the value that you have generated is to create a survey that will help you quantify Power's goals and translate them into cost savings and revenue generation. The survey should verify the savings opportunities that exist in your solution. As you create your survey, investigate how your industry trade association describes the value of the product or service you provide. Then take that concept and customize it to the specific product or solution you offer.

Every company's survey will be different because it will be based on its product and industry. But there are some general types of information you should be trying to gather to help you understand the very specific value you've been able to create.

- Basic data about the company, including industry, annual revenue, and total annual expenditure in the area of your solution or product, are key pieces of information to use in building your model.

- Look at savings data—including savings the company expected to and actually achieved by using your product. Provide a list of specific areas in which savings may be based on knowledge of your product, but allow the company the opportunity to elaborate. This will help you identify your value drivers.

- Gather feedback about why the company bought your solution. You may already have this information from the clients you are surveying, but if not, this is a great time to gather it. Try listing the pain points you've defined for your product so far.

What you want to create from the survey process is a clear definition of how your product drives value for your customers—both direct value (bottom line) and indirect value (productivity enhancements). We call these elements your value drivers. You will likely start the survey process with a hypothesis of what you believe to be the value you create, and you will use that hypothesis to help you create the survey. The survey will then help you refine your claims and back them up with customers' quantifiable results and quotations. In the end, the greater part of your sales message will be pulled directly from your customers. You can use the data you gather to turn your sales force into messengers of the customers' ideas and achieved value rather than messengers and proponents of their own ideas and interpretations.

You will turn your sales force into messengers of your customers' ideas and achieved value.

You'll have to spend the time to carefully construct this survey and refine it. You need very specific information from your customers, and you need to come away from the survey process with a clear idea of how your product drives value for them. It's crucial that the value drivers you develop are not exactly like your competitors'; they need to be specific to your solution. You want to prove the value of *your* solution, not any solution.

WAKE-UP CALL

The more complex your product or solution, the more you'll want to look for the big-picture savings you create. Contrary to old-school techniques designed to extract every minute detail of your value, you should be looking for the larger, more Power-relevant contributors to value. Why? Because our goal is to partner with Power's process owners and verify your value claim in one to two business days, and that can be done only if you are focused on the large-scope value, not the minutiae.

In the sample survey shown here, Kurt has used the information he's gathered so far about his customers and his Zebra to help him discover his value drivers. Comments in brackets indicate how to structure your own survey.

Once you have a preliminary survey prepared, send it to a couple of your best customers. Then follow up with a phone call and interview them. You'll be able to review the survey for ambiguity or questions that lead to generalized rather than specific answers. Correct the ambiguity to ensure consistent responses, and then continue to conduct your surveys with all the Zebras you've identified within your customer base.

As part of the survey process, you will track the lowest and highest reported level of savings for each component of your value drivers. After correcting for or eliminating any obviously wrong responses (extreme outliers), you will use the lower end of the value claims to build your value prediction model (because the lower end offers conservative results) and the higher end as an

C3 Customer Survey

Profile Information

Company Name: _____

Last Name:_____ First Name:_____ Role/Title:_____

E-mail Address:_____

Which department do you report to?

☐ CEO's office

☐ Finance   ☐ Sales

☐ Production   ☐ Human resources

☐ Procurement   ☐ Distribution

☐ Marketing   ☐ _____

Please indicate your industry (SIC code[s]). [List the industries you typically operate in.]

☐ Pharmaceutical   ☐ Manufacturing

☐ Health care   ☐ Consumer product goods

☐ Financial services   ☐ Retail

☐ Wholesale/distribution   ☐ High tech

☐ Professional services   ☐ Oil and gas

☐ Utilities   ☐ Government

☐ Other _____

Please indicate the entity for which you will be providing financial information throughout the survey.   ☐ Global   ☐ US   ☐ One or more division(s)

Total annual revenues of your company: _____

Total annual expenditure associated with the movement of goods in your supply chain—within your warehouse and production environment: _____ [Indicate what area your product or solution typically falls under.]

Total annual number of full-time equivalents (FTEs) who work on your supply chain (this should include all customer service personnel who work directly with customers): _____

Total number of FTEs using the C3 solution: _____

Annual average salary plus benefits of supply-chain personnel: _____

Tasks outsourced to third parties at a cost of: _____

Savings Data

Did you create a capital appropriation request or similar internal documentation to get funding for this initiative?   ☐ Yes   ☐ No

We have found through our research that companies such as yours have purchased the C3 solution for the following business reasons. Please check all that apply to you. [List the pain points you've identified in your customer base.]

_____ Ability to address customer-initiated change (example: two-day delivery of custom product that used to take two weeks) to help spur growth

_____ Increase customer loyalty to increase sales to existing customers

_____ Ability to address industry-initiated change (better business-to-business-based connection to your suppliers, improving accuracy and reducing the cycle time it takes to get deliveries) to accelerate growth

_____ Better use of existing assets (C3 solution continues to move product even after the business has closed) to reduce costs

_____ Improve efficiency and overall efficacy

_____ Improve compliance or reduce risk

_____ Other (please specify) _____

_____ Other (please specify) _____

_____ Other (please specify) _____

Direct cost savings: Projected: _____   Actual: _____

Please specify the source of the savings, scoring all that apply:

Increased inventory returns and shrinkage reductions

1. _____ Reduction in waste or scrap (Score 4 = yes, 2 = in process, 0 = no)
   Amount saved $_____

2. _____ Reduction in damaged goods (Score 4 = yes, 2 = in process, 0 = no)
   Amount saved $_____

3. _____ Frequent but smaller inventory releases (Score 4 = yes, 2 = in process, 0 = no)
   Amount saved $_____

4. _____ Reduction in lost or stolen items (Score 4 = yes, 2 = in process, 0 = no)
   Amount saved $_____

5. _____ Increase in inventory turns (Score 4 = yes, 2 = in process, 0 = no)
   Amount saved $_____

Lean labor, speed, and scalability

6. _____ Reduction in FTEs required to move goods to the shop floor
   (Score 6 = yes, 3 = in process, 0 = no)
   Amount saved $_____

7. _____ Reduction in FTEs needed to move goods from production to inventory
   (Score 6 = yes, 3 = in process, 0 = no)
   Amount saved $_____

8. _____ Less time spent in material requirements planning
   (Score 6 = yes, 3 = in process, 0 = no)
   Amount saved $_____

Material process effectiveness

9. _____ Less time to produce finished goods (Score 6 = yes, 3 = in process, 0 = no)
   Amount saved $_____

10. _____ Materials delivered when and as they are needed (eliminate safety stock)
    (Score 6 = yes, 3 = in process, 0 = no)
    Amount saved $_____

11. _____ Finished goods put away and handled only once
    (Score 6 = yes, 3 = in process, 0 = no)
    Amount saved $_____

Outsourcing service and analytics

12. _____ Elimination of direct employees (outsourced supply-chain employees to C3)
    (Score 12 = yes, 6 = in process, 0 = no)
    Amount saved $_____

Process Maturity

Projects that have buy-in and support from the executive level of an organization tend to mature, grow in importance, and achieve their goals. The ability to tie results of a project into corporate goals, earnings-per-share contribution, or other important metrics generally helps to drive the desired results. Please help us understand if your C3 initiative has executive-level support.

13. _____ Does this program have specific goals? (Score 6 = yes, 3 = in process, 0 = no)

14. _____ Are you the executive who owns the promises that led to the approval of this project? (Score 6 = yes, 3 = in process, 0 = no)

15. _____ Are there still tangible measures in place to track the project?
    (Score 6 = yes, 3 = in process, 0 = no)

example of best-in-class results achievable through the use of a best-practice approach. Later in the chapter we'll explain how you'll use the scores the customer provided to create conservative value estimates and powerful sales tools. We discuss the ways you will leverage both the low end and the high end of your predicted range of value in chapter 7.

 WAKE-UP CALL

If you are selling in multiple industries, your goal is to gather responses from at least three customers per industry. One customer documenting a certain level of value is a fact. Two customers in the same vertical verifying the value is a pattern. Three customers in the same vertical verifying the value is a trend. The CFO or his or her designate should verify all financial value claims.

So what might your value drivers look like? Well, they will be different for every company, but in broad terms they tend to be similar within industries. Your solution probably increases revenue, reduces costs, or allows people to be more productive, freeing them to address the important issues rather than the mundane and repetitive aspects of their jobs. By reducing waste, reducing time, or increasing efficiency, more can be done with less. When you help companies continuously improve, you drive value. Quantifying that value earns you the right to sell your message to Power.

The important thing to consider when identifying your value drivers is the specifics in each of the broad areas: *How* does *your* product drive savings and *what* are those savings? Some of the value you generate will be direct and some will be indirect (see the box "Finance for Salespeople 102" on page 119). For each value driver, you need to specify what type of savings are generated and how those savings translate into adjustments to the bottom line. Based on your analysis of survey data, you might develop a table like the one below, where the percentage of savings translates into decreased expenditures in the area of your product or solution. While the percentages seem miniscule, the company in this example has customers that spend millions each year in their area, so the resulting overall savings in dollar amounts are quite high.

Create efficiency through automating manual processes	
• Reduced time spent sourcing in given area	• Indirect savings of 0.53%
• Registration website outsourcing cost reduction	• Direct savings of 1.62%
• Reduction in management tasks	• Indirect savings of 0.22%
Sourcing/procurement	
• Vendor consolidation and the preferred supplier program	• Direct savings of 1.34%
• Negotiated discounts in costs in given area	• Direct savings of 0.16%
Enhance visibility and control	
• Tighten approvals and implement clear policies on spending	• Direct savings of 0.62%
• Cost savings from reducing paperwork	• Indirect savings of 0.12%

We could write an entire book about how to uncover the value of your product, but in this book the most important lessons are: follow the leads from your research, and be as specific as possible in order to differentiate your solution from your competitors'.

Finance for Salespeople 102

DIRECT SAVINGS VERSUS INDIRECT SAVINGS: Direct savings are hard-cost reductions. A dollar of direct savings is a dollar that goes directly to the bottom line (contributes to earnings before interest and taxes, or EBIT). Indirect savings are savings and revenue generated from areas such as productivity gains. CFOs will sometimes prevent you from including indirect savings or productivity improvements in various CAR calculations because they are harder to definitively quantify. Nonetheless, indirect savings should in many cases still be added to direct savings to calculate the expected project benefit.

EARNINGS BEFORE INTEREST AND TAXES: EBIT is what financial people use to measure your solution's value or contribution to profit. For example, if your solution generates labor cost savings of $1, that $1 is a direct contribution to EBIT. If your solution improves productivity, there may be a direct or an indirect contribution to EBIT because your solution helps directly increase sales, and indirectly reduces costs. The $1 of sales increase has to be reduced by material, labor, and other costs required to produce and sell that $1 of product. So $1 in sales increase reduced by costs leaves us with something less, perhaps $0.10. The $0.10 would be the direct contribution to EBIT. If your solution allows the same number of people to do more work, there is an indirect contribution to EBIT. Why indirect? Because your prospect will still pay their more productive people the same amount, before and after implementation of your solution.

TOTAL COST OF OWNERSHIP: A TCO is a financial estimate designed to help assess direct and indirect costs related to the purchase of any capital investment. It is a form of full-cost accounting limited to costs clearly associated with a given solution. A TCO assessment ideally offers a final statement reflecting not only the cost of the purchase but also all aspects in the further use and maintenance of the solution considered. This includes the cost of training support personnel and the users of the system, and more. For example, the decision to buy a given solution may result in the following TCO analysis: the greater initial price of a high-end solution after including all costs—implementation, product, training, consulting, change management, and cost of capital—should be balanced by adding likely repair costs and earlier replacement to the purchase cost of the cheaper bargain brand. As you can see, the initial price becomes just the beginning of the life cycle of costs.

Once you have defined your value drivers, explored the specific components of those drivers that comprise the value, and determined how each of those elements affects the bottom line, you are well on your way to creating one of the best sales tools you'll ever use.

Kurt has worked the process of determining his value drivers very quickly. He didn't really have a choice; his meeting with Mark Nem is tomorrow and he has to make it work for C3. He knows that if they really lose Nem's, he might as well start packing up his office.

Kent was helpful and shared the survey that his division had used. Kurt used that survey as a foundation and adapted it based on his team's research. He knew some of the key areas in which his customers had achieved savings, but he didn't really know what those savings looked like. Kurt didn't have time to go to every one of his Zebra customers, but he went to the top six, pulled in some favors, and got the surveys back fast. And thank goodness he did, because the results were incredibly informative.

Based on the results from the surveys and some quick number crunching, Kurt has developed the following value drivers. (His information is limited to those value drivers that result in direct reductions in supply-chain costs.)

Increased inventory turns and shrinkage reductions

• Automation of frequent but smaller inventory releases	• Direct savings of 2.150%
• Less handling of materials reduces chance of damage	• Direct savings of 1.250%

Lean labor, speed, and scalability

• Fewer FTEs required to move goods to shop floor	• Direct savings of 0.150%
• Fewer FTEs to move goods from production to inventory	• Direct savings of 0.075%
• Less time spent in material requirements planning	• Direct savings of 0.100%

Material process effectiveness

• Less time to produce finished goods	• Direct savings of 0.003%
• Materials delivered when and as needed (eliminate safety stock)	• Direct savings of 0.050%
• Finished goods put away and handled only once	• Direct savings of 0.050%

Outsourcing service and analytics

• Elimination of direct employees (outsourced to C3 payroll)	• Direct savings of 1.000%

Kurt is excited to plug some information into the ROI model that Kent sent to him.

PREDICTING YOUR VALUE

Okay, you've gone through the task of gathering specific data from your customers and quantifying your value drivers. So what do you do with these data now?

Using the data you've gathered (and some more that we'll outline next), you will be able to create a financial model that supports your Zebra efforts. The characteristics of a Zebra are important, but if you can't quantify the value you can generate for your Zebra, all of your research won't convince prospects that you are a perfect fit for them. Power needs financial proof of the value you say you've created for other customers—and that you can do it for his company.

 WAKE-UP CALL

Keep in mind that your ultimate goal is not to justify a solution, but to justify and sell *your* solution. Many companies have an ROI model that justifies a decision to buy a solution, any solution—even the solutions their competitors are offering. The ROI data we'll help you produce will specifically justify your solution because they will be based on your specific value drivers.

On our website, sellingtozebras.com, the Zebra University section allows you to access a template of the model we have created to help you synthesize your data into a single, powerful analytical tool. This tool will help you determine how much value you can create for a prospect, and it will generate graphics that will convince Power that you have something special to offer. Download the Microsoft Excel file Waterfall Value Model. In the file, we've provided step-by-step instructions for customizing the model for your business. This book isn't long enough for us to give you a detailed description of how we built the model, so we're just going to give it to you and explain the basics of how to use it. Here we'll outline the information you need to gather and how it ties in to the spreadsheet. But know that the model is powerful because it is based on years of helping clients predict, verify, and present their predictive and verified value to executives in a position of Power, all over the world!

The model is based on the assumption that you will be able to replicate the value you have created for your customers by addressing executive-level business issues for your prospects. Your prospects, however, must have similar business issues, be of similar size in terms of revenues and/or employee numbers, and be in the same or similar type of business (industry and SIC code). The template we've provided is purposely simple. Keeping the inputs basic means salespeople get excited about it and will actually use it. The model does all the heavy lifting for you: the financial calculations, the graphical output, and most importantly, the prediction of the value that your product or solution will be able to generate for the prospect.

 You can predict value for a prospect on the assumption that you will be able to replicate the value you have created for your customers who are in the same industry, are of a similar size, and have similar business issues.

You've already pulled together most of the data you need to create a powerful ROI model, particularly if you use our template. The value drivers with savings percentages create the basis of the model. From there you just have to fill in the pieces of information described in the following paragraphs.

Information about the prospect: You need only three key pieces of information about the prospect, and they are usually easy to get: industry, annual revenue, and annual expenditure in the area of your solution or product. You'll see in the template that if the company is a public company, you can fill in more information on earnings, outstanding shares, and so on, but these three pieces of data are key to using the tool.

The required investment: Use a robust estimate of the investment in your solution required to achieve the results that others have obtained. Go high with your estimate. Include everything needed to achieve the level of value you will position to Power. At this point in the process, Power will not focus on your price. Power will focus on the results you claim to deliver! A robust solution investment also reduces your value claim by this same amount, making your value prediction that much more conservative. (Hint: that's a good thing!)

The discount rate for both NPV and EVA calculations will automatically be provided for you, or you can set your own: See the boxes "Finance for Salespeople 101" and "Finance for Salespeople 102" (pages 97 and 119) if you need a reminder of what these calculations mean and how they are used. The model uses the higher of the prospect's operating margin or 10 percent to be as conservative as possible. You can also adjust the percentage based on your own assessment of the financial environment, including the rate of return for any other projects the prospect is considering investing in.

Ramp-up information: The ramp-up is your estimate of the time it will take to implement your solution fully (not to be confused with implementation time) and achieve 100 percent of the benefits you claim are possible. So the benefits for each twelve-month use of your solution will be reduced by how you set the ramp-up period in the model. For example, if you think it will take three years, the company may achieve only 50 percent of the benefit the first year they use your product or solution, 75 percent the second year, and 100 percent the third year. By ramping the expected benefits, it is clear to Power that you aren't saying that the moment your solution is in place, the savings are going to come flooding in. It shows that you're smart, realistic, and honest—three characteristics that Power values! Be conservative with these estimates to set realistic expectations and strengthen your claim.

Process maturity information: Most of your prospects will have partial solutions in place to deal with the business issues you address. So some of the possible benefit you claim may have been realized already. The survey you conducted will help you understand how much value your customers have already achieved from your solution or from other solutions they have in place. But how do you determine and use this information for prospects?

In the model we've provided, we've standardized the value reductions by providing percentages (0, 25, 50, or 75 percent) for you to select for each primary value driver. The higher the percentage you select, the more conservative your value claim. For example, if you select the 25 percent quartile for one of your value drivers, you are moving that 25 percent into the preexisting benefits area and reducing the value your solution can generate by 25 percent.

You may not have much information about the value a prospect has already achieved when you first use the model (before you've met with Power), so you'll have to use some rough estimates based on what you know of the company. Again be conservative. When in doubt, assume they have achieved savings with their older, less-capable solution. Do a preliminary run-through of the survey for a prospect based on any information you can gather. You'll be able to use the scores to better determine how much value they are already achieving with the solutions they have in place and how to adjust your value claims.

As shown in the sample customer survey on pages 115 and 116, you should ask your customers to assign point scores for specific questions related to your value drivers, generating scores based on how far they've come in achieving maximum value from your solution or others. In the sample survey, the scored questions relate specifically to the value drivers Kurt determined for his solutions (i.e., questions 1 through 5 relate to his first value driver). If you structure your survey this way, you can tally the scores for each group of questions and use those scores to determine how to adjust your value claims to reflect the preexisting benefits within a customer or prospect.

As an example, in Kurt's survey, the scoring would look like this:

Value Driver 1		Value Driver 2		Value Driver 3		Value Driver 4	
total score		total score		total score		total score	
0–8:	0%	0–6:	0%	0–8:	0%	0:	0%
9–12:	2%	7–10:	25%	9–12:	25%	6:	25%
13–16:	50%	11–14:	50%	13–16:	50%	12:	50%
17–20:	75%	15–18:	75%	17–18:	75%		

You'll use these scores again later to generate a critical sales tool, and we'll show you how to leverage this preexisting benefits information in a powerful way in chapters 7 and 8.

Building and Using Your Model

One of the keys to the success of the Zebra way of predicting value, and to the uniqueness of this process, is your ability to demonstrate that all your value claims are conservative and very achievable. This starts with the way you set the possible value for each value driver. As we said, when you gather information from your customers with the survey, you'll track the lowest and highest value created by various customers. When you input the information into the spreadsheet, you'll use the lowest values (low-end prediction) to keep your overall prediction of value conservative and achievable.

The model is built in Microsoft Excel, which allows you to attach comments to cells or data (as we discussed in the explanation of the Push-button Zebra). Attach a comment to each value driver you enter into the model, explaining that the lowest savings any customer reported in your survey is the savings prediction you used for that value driver. You should also mention the highest savings as the best-in-class reported result. Finally, you should explain how your solution creates this value. This is how you tie this value-generation ability specifically to *your* solution—not just any solution. And you'll need this information as you continue through the Zebra Buying Cycle.

Lean Labor, Speed, Scalability	Savings / Benefit	% Reduction	Type	
Fewer FTE's required to move goods to shop floor	$345,600	0.150%	Direct	Indirect
Fewer FTEs needed to move good from production to inventory	$172,800	0.075%	Direct	Indirect
Less time spent in material requirements planning	$2,304,000	1.000%	Direct	Indirect
	$0	0.000%	Direct	Indirect
Annual SUBTOTAL for Lean Labor, Speed, Scalability	$2,822,400	including Direct & Indirect Savings		

Value Driver Information in the Zebra ROI Model

Here is a sample of a value driver from Kurt's value model—"Lean Labor, speed, and scalability." To the line item "Fewer FTEs [full-time equivalents] required to move goods to the shop floor," Kurt has attached the following comment:

Assumption: Results from question 7 of the C3 Customer Survey showed a low of 0.150 percent savings of total supply-chain expenditures and a best-practice high of 0.30 percent.

Calculation: C3 customers have 11.1 FTEs for material movement per $1B in annual revenue. C3 customers reported a reduction of material movement

FTEs of between 3 percent and 6 percent. The average material movement FTE annual salary, including benefits, is $46,500.

FTEs × 0.3 = number of FTE reductions

number of FTE reductions × $46,500/total supply-chain expenditure = percent savings in total supply-chain expenditure from this value driver

This formula translates into an average savings of between 0.15% and 0.30% of total supply-chain expenditure. We used the low end of our range (0.150%) to calculate the productivity increase associated with the C3 solution. But a best-practice customer achieved savings of 0.30% of total supply-chain expenditure.

C3 produces this result by: Pickup documentation and radio frequency devices on materials and handheld locator devices provide fork truck operators with everything they need to quickly locate target goods. Once pickup is made, the driver updates documentation using the handheld device. Documentation is electronic and accurate. Items are handled once. Labor expense is reduced.

The other way to keep your prediction of value conservative is to set the preexisting benefits percentages high. For example, Kurt knows Nem's is using older pieces of the C3 solution purchased a number of years ago, so he has moved them to quartile 2 for the "Increased inventory turns and shrinkage reductions," "Material process effectiveness," and "Outsourcing service and analytics" value drivers. This shifts 25 percent of the potential benefits into the preexisting benefits column. How does he know this? Kurt has completed the survey he created on Nem's behalf. His answers will have to be verified and corroborated with managers that Mark Nem trusts, but this first pass allows him to create a prediction of value he can use to reconnect with Nem's at the Power level, with Mark Nem. And it allows him to set the preexisting benefit parameters. Nem's scored fairly low in each category (for each value driver), so Kurt is able to set the percentage to 25 percent for the first three value drivers and 0 for the last, at least preliminarily.

Waterfall Controls					Preexisting Benefits	C3 Benefit
	Select appropriate quartile of "Process Maturity" for each value driver below					
Increased Inventory Returns & Shrinkage Reduction	Quartile 1 - 0%	Quartile 2 - 25%	Quartile 3 - 50%	Quartile 4 - 75%	25%	75%
Lean Labor, Speed, Scalability	Quartile 1 - 0%	Quartile 2 - 25%	Quartile 3 - 50%	Quartile 4 - 75%	25%	75%
Material Process Effectiveness	Quartile 1 - 0%	Quartile 2 - 25%	Quartile 3 - 50%	Quartile 4 - 75%	25%	75%
Outsourcing Service & Analytics	Quartile 1 - 0%	Quartile 2 - 25%	Quartile 3 - 50%	Quartile 4 - 75%	0%	100%

Setting Preexisting Benefits Parameters in the Zebra ROI Model

Finally, you can change your ramp-up percentages to change the time frame for achieving full benefits. For Kurt, it might be smart to set the ramp-up claims very low, proving his desire to set expectations of value at a level he knows he can help Mark Nem and his people achieve. If Kurt sets them as we have in our example, at 40 percent, 75 percent, and 90 percent over the first three years, he will be able to look Mark Nem in the eye and claim he has very conservatively set the expectations because the value claim in year one is only 40 percent of the total, year two is 75 percent of the total, and so on.

Waterfall Ramp-up	2008/2009	2009/2010	2010/2011	2011/2012	2012/2013
	40%	75%	90%	100%	100%

The Ramp-up in the Zebra ROI Model

When you are done with your model, you will also create a Microsoft Word document (we call this "the discovery document") that mirrors your value model. The text document will contain each value driver and any notes (like the one Kurt wrote) about each one. This way you won't have to use the model directly with the prospect during later stages of the Zebra Buying Cycle; rather, you can use the text document, which is usually easier.

POWER-LEVEL SALES TOOLS

Using the model you've created from customer data and the prospect information, you can now predict the value you will create for your prospect. How you present that prediction of value is just as important as the validity of the prediction. You could give Power a host of spreadsheets with detailed information about your company and theirs, or you could distill that information to make better use of their time and yours. What do you think would be most effective?

In the Zebra model, you generate three sales tools once you input your data: critical financials, the Value Waterfall (possibly the most important tool), and the payback period graph. These are the only tools you'll need to explain to Power, in his language, how your product drives value as you solve the company's business problems. A fourth tool, the achieved-value radar diagram, can be generated for existing clients to help them see what additional value can be gained from your solutions.

Financials

The model automatically calculates Power-level financials to use in communicating the predicted value generated by your solution. These are the numbers Power wants to see, so you must be prepared to discuss them. And while beauty isn't everything, attractive, clear graphics will help you leverage this wealth of financial information.

3-Year Results -- Direct & Indirect Savings	
EBIT Impact	$17.92M
P&L Impact	$11.64M
Payback Period	9 Months
Cost of Indecision	$497,643 per month

Financials Proving Your Value

In the sample shown above, Kurt's prediction of value for Nem's is based on four key pieces of financial data:

- **EBIT impact:** After accounting for all the costs (including the cost of their own people), the project will generate more than $17 million of earnings before interest and taxes over three years.
- **P&L impact:** The project will contribute more than $11 million to profit over three years.
- **Payback period:** Nem's will have all of its money back after just nine months.
- **Cost of indecision:** If Nem's decides not to go with the C3 solution, they will lose almost $500,000 per month, every month they don't have the solution installed.

Can you see how valuable this information is? When you generate data like these, and learn to talk with credibility and conviction, you will have learned the language of Power!

 WAKE-UP CALL

As we've discussed, you are competing for every dollar of available capital with every other possible use of the capital. No matter how your prospect chooses to evaluate capital projects, you must provide everything necessary to understand that an investment in your solution stacks up well against other uses of that same capital.

The Value Waterfall

While the financials show the overall results a company can expect from a project, they won't necessarily hit Power's hot buttons, or pain points. Those financial numbers, while important, don't explain your value drivers, or how those value drivers address Power's pain points. That's why the Value Waterfall might be the most important sales tool you'll ever use. In one quick step, you can show, in a quantifiable way, the specific and unique value of your solution, and why Power should care. In short, the Value Waterfall will help you differentiate your product or solution and get to Power. Yes, it appears to be a backward waterfall. We call it a waterfall because the value cascades, or builds, pillar by pillar.

The Value Waterfall functionally is a graphical representation of value created by the various functional components of your solution. Each pillar, or column, represents one of your value drivers—a component of your solution that you've found to generate a quantifiable value for your clients of similar size and

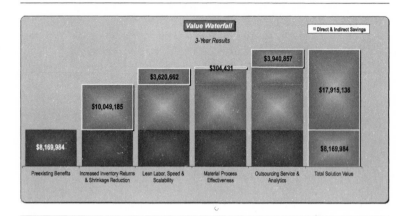

Value Waterfall

industry. Kurt's Value Waterfall for Nem's shows that C3 predicts it can generate about $10 million by increasing inventory turns and reducing inventory shrinkage and $3.6 million by supporting process improvements required by Nem's lean manufacturing initiative (a particularly powerful claim, given that Nem's stated corporate direction is to reduce costs by implementing a lean initiative). A lesser amount of three hundred thousand dollars is generated through better material process execution. And finally, through the use of outsourcing and analytics-driven metrics, C3 will drive $3.9 million of value. Ultimately, Kurt will be able to present to Mark Nem a solution that will generate $17.9 million in savings over a three-year period. And that's not something that most people in a position of power will ignore.

The amazing thing about the Value Waterfall is that it can be used in so many ways during the sales process, particularly if you're following the Zebra path:

- Get access to Power, who is interested in proven value.
- Strengthen your negotiating position because of the value you have quantified (will help reduce discounting).
- Sell more products to existing customers (you can offer to do a customer audit and make recommendations for how to get more from the investment they've already made in your product and discover additional consulting, education, or products to help produce more value).
- Differentiate your solution from competition.
- Ensure that you sell your solution properly so you are able to, and get paid to, Force Success.
- Establish your company/sales team as thought leaders in your space.
- Turn customer-driven sales cycles into Zebra Buying Cycles.
- Establish clear metrics of success to help drive implementation in the proper direction.

Payback Period Graph

Our ROI model presents the payback period in terms of months in the financial data section. Because payback period is so closely aligned with risk, the model automatically produces a payback-period graph so you can demonstrate, dramatically, that your solution is low risk.

Kurt's graph for Nem's helps demonstrate that the C3 solution is particularly low risk, with a payback period of just nine months. The steeply sloped line shows the strong savings projection predicted for the C3 solution. Notice that the monthly project gross line crosses the monthly solution costs line in month nine.

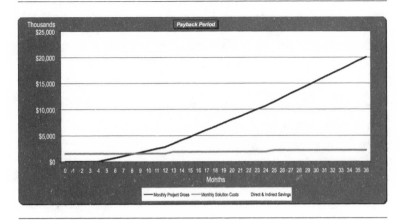

Payback Period

The Achieved-Value Radar Diagram

The achieved-value radar diagram is a unique way of reaching Power in your current customer base, to reinvigorate your relationship, to approach Power with new products and services, or to Force Success. What the value radar shows is how much value the customer has achieved with your products and services that are currently in place. But, more importantly, it offers an immediate comparison to the value that others have achieved with your solutions, letting Power know if there is more value to be gained. This will allow you to talk about upgrades, services, or even internal process improvements that could extract more value from products or services already in use. This is going to be amazingly appealing to Power, because you'll be presenting a low-cost way to get a much greater ROI. And it shows Power that you're invested in the success of your customers. And who wouldn't want to work with a company like that?!

So, how is the achieved-value radar generated? From the survey data, of course. Remember the scores tallied from the survey questions? Well, now you can use those scores to generate an achieved-value radar diagram. In the model, you will also enter data indicating the highest possible scores that can be achieved with your solution, the highest scores your very best customers have been able to achieve, and the highest scores your best customers in each industry segment have been able to achieve. These scores will allow you to compare the prospect's or customer's scores to what's possible. Once you enter these data, you'll be able to generate the diagram shown here.

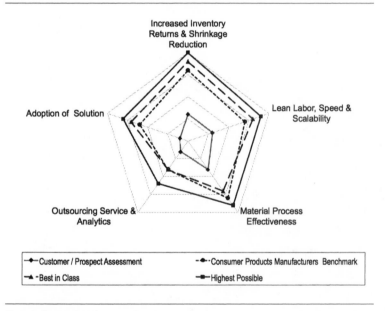

The Achieved-Value Radar Diagram

Note that the radar has one additional spoke that is not one of the key value drivers. The "Adoption of Solution" spoke is generated by the total score for the "Process Maturity" questions (13 through 15) in the sample survey. This is a helpful spoke in determining the present and future success of a project, particularly because as you implement a solution with a new client, you can continuously update this diagram to show them, in a very visual and powerful way, how they're progressing toward the maximum value achievable. The figure shown on page 136 is based on Kurt's analysis of Nem's, which hasn't adopted the new solution C3 is proposing, so that score is currently 0. Doesn't this figure present a dramatic tool for Kurt to present to Mark Nem? It can be a powerful tool for you, too!

This chapter presented some heavy-duty information about value drivers, financial data, and predicting ROI. This is probably the toughest part of the Zebra way for most salespeople or sales managers. In the past it hasn't been easy to define in very specific, quantifiable terms the value you're going to create. But if you can do this—and we have made it considerably easier to accomplish this task—you have at your fingertips everything you need to sell to Power. And you have to do the tough stuff only once. After that, it's just filling in bits of information. Soon you'll be predicting value for prospects in fifteen minutes or less!

PARTNER WITH YOUR ZEBRA

CHAPTER 6

MEET WITH POWER

DID YOU EVER GET TO THE END OF A SALES CYCLE only to find that the enthusiastic non–decision makers couldn't help you get a deal done, in spite of their best efforts? Many salespeople have experienced this: The person you've been relying on to sell your solution to upper management didn't know what they didn't know—what it would take to get a buy order approved inside their own company.

It can be difficult for salespeople to get appointments, much less appointments with real decision makers. So it's hard to say no when the first appointment is with somebody other than the final decision maker. But this is exactly what you have to do. One factor that contributes to the tendency to say yes when you should say no is the activity-for-activity's-sake approach, or using hustle as a way to make up for formulating and executing on a truly effective strategy. And because of this frequently practiced but time-wasting approach, decision makers know that in all probability, a meeting with a sales rep is going to be a waste of their time.

WAKE-UP CALL

Getting meetings with prospects is hard, and getting meetings with high-level decision makers is particularly hard. But if you don't get that meeting, you may be wasting your time with the prospect anyway. If you can't sell to Power, you may not be able to sell at all. Follow the GHorSH motto: Go High or Stay Home, or you'll be saying, "GHorSH, I wish I'd done that!" Penetrating Power effectively takes practice, discipline, and persistence, but it is a critical component in advancing the Zebra Buying Cycle to the next step.

Just as your prospects aren't experts at implementing your solutions, they aren't experts at buying what you're selling either. Because of repeated experience, you and your company probably know who should buy your products and how they should be bought: the way that creates the most mutual value for your customer and you. Prospects haven't gone through the dozens or hundreds of sales cycles you may have experienced in selling your solution, so they don't know how best to buy a solution like yours. And if you approach a deal at the middle-management level, you can't expect middle management to know how to sell your solutions to their own upper management as well as you can. Deals that die or take months, quarters, or even years to close are a result of selling at too low a level. This is why it is critical for you to begin working at the executive level, and maintain that through the entire cycle.

This is the origin of necessity from which the Zebra Buying Cycle was born! It helps you identify those accounts you should be pursuing, ensures that you're spending time and resources fruitfully, and gives you the tools to sell at the executive level.

When you request a meeting with Power at a prospect you believe is a Zebra, you must provide her with everything she needs to decide to grant you that meeting. So far, we've given you all the tools you'll need to uncover the value you can create for a prospect account and communicate that value in very specific terms. But, because getting the first appointment with Power is so important, we're going to show you how to get to Power and sell that value. Remember, people at the Power level are decision makers, so if you don't give them what they need to give you a yes, you'll get a no. If you've followed the Zebra path outlined so far, you should have what you need already, and you probably even have what you need for the meeting itself. But how do you get that meeting?

HOW TO GET POWER ON THE PHONE

The hardest part of getting a meeting with Power may be just getting him on the phone and willing to talk to you. There are books in the market that offer some helpful dos and don'ts, but today, Power is often guarded by an almost impenetrable voice-mail system. Some companies even make you fill out an online vendor profile that is forwarded to the purchasing department for screening before they will connect you beyond the switchboard. Suddenly, you're stuck in purgatory many levels below Power before you're even out of the gate.

Let's review a proven approach that works in today's highly competitive pursuit for Power's share of mind.

- Uncover the names of executives who might be Power (at least three executives to pursue).

- Send e-mail to at least three potential Power-level contacts to pave the way.
- In all communications, mention the other two executives you are pursuing.
- Conduct a voice-mail campaign, leaving something of value with each message.
- Prepare an executive brief that you can send if necessary.

 WAKE-UP CALL

- It usually takes about seven phone calls to talk with an executive at a Global 2000 company.

- You will be relegated and delegated to the management level that matches the image you project in those calls.

Who to Contact First

If you do not currently have access to Power at a prospect or even within your customer base, which is not unlikely if you have been living in a pre-Zebra world, the best way to get access to Power is to call the assistant to the CEO. Why the assistant to the CEO? CEO assistants often have tremendous power and knowledge. Many CEO assistants have outlasted two or more CEOs. They know the inner workings of their company, are intelligent, and know most of the Power-level people in the organization well. Therefore, they are the best resources for information in the organization, regardless of its size.

Think of the assistant to the CEO as Power. The way you present yourself is the key to your effectiveness. The assistant guards the CEO's time with verve and has lots of practice dispatching salespeople and others who are viewed as time wasters. Assistants are also excellent judges of character, so if you exhibit even the least bit of condescension in your approach, they will recognize it, and you will be relegated down or even out.

First and foremost, the assistant to the CEO deserves to be treated with the utmost respect. Treat the assistant to the CEO with the same respect you would the CEO and you'll get what you need. With effective use of this approach, skilled sales representatives often have been provided with an introduction to Power courtesy of the CEO's assistant. They have even been granted the privilege of booking an appointment with Power without ever having a direct preliminary conversation.

 WAKE-UP CALL

Remember, you are looking for Power, but Power is not necessarily the CEO. Depending on your product or level of value, Power may be a vice president of a particular division. It might not be appropriate to seek a C-level appointment. If that is the case, don't try. Your objective here is to find the right person, not the highest-level person you can possibly reach, and then pursue an appointment.

To make this process work for you, to gain the trust and help of the assistant to the CEO, you must be able to do the following:

- Quickly answer the question, "What does your company do?"
- Quickly answer the question, "Why are you calling me?"
- Do not allow yourself to be delegated back to middle management—explain why there is value for the prospect if you meet with an executive.

- Reference the research you've done to earn the right to speak with an executive, which will help demonstrate why your message is an executive-level message.

To help you do all of these things effectively, we recommend you create a script for calls to these assistants.

When you are on the phone with the assistant to the CEO, you should be trying to get the names of at least three potential Powers and an introduction to at least one. When you pursue multiple executives, you create an internal awareness of your company and maybe even a sense of competition. If one exec asks another about your company, she'll want to be able to respond intelligently, and that may be to your advantage.

Get approval from the assistant to say that you got the names from him. This will give you greater credibility when you call these individuals. Power will respect that you took this step first to find the right person to contact.

What if you already have access to Power, particularly at a client company? That's great. If so, you can bypass this step and go directly to calling Power.

While Kurt has been very focused on the Nem's account, he knows he has an incredible amount of research compiled that he needs to start leveraging with other prospects. He can't rely on Nem's to pull his division out of the fire. Kurt believes he knows who Power is at Costline Food Group, a new prospect that got an initial Z-score of 17. But Kurt is missing some information, and he thinks that the score will end up being much higher. He decides to contact the assistant to the CEO first to confirm his information about Power—and maybe even get an introduction. The assistant's name is Patricia Jones.

"Hello, Patricia, my name is Kurt Kustner. I am with C3, and we provide supply-chain solutions. We are the thought and solution leaders in the supply-chain space. We have launched a benchmarking program based on industry and best-in-class practices, which we have gathered from our extensive customer base. I have researched Costline and learned that you are similar to some of my customers because you have a company-wide initiative called "Customer first to gain market share." So, we have created a prediction of value for Costline that is based on that same benchmark data from our customers. If we solve the same types of pain points for you that we have solved in the past, we will generate about $21 million in value for Costline over the next three years. Who would be the most appropriate executives to contact at Costline to discuss this value?"

"Did you say your name was Kurt?" Patricia asks.

"Yes."

"Kurt, what is it C3 does, exactly?"

Kurt frames his response in terms of what C3 can do for Costline. "We provide people, processes, and technology that can improve the efficiency of ordering and delivering products at Costline."

"Why aren't you talking to managers in our supply-chain department?"

"As part of our process we will speak with managers in your supply-chain department, but our solution touches many different departments, including finance, purchasing, and logistics. The customers who receive the most value from our solution allow us to talk to the executive who is in charge of all of these areas. Could you tell me who the executive in charge might be?"

"Well, I'm not sure. But why are you calling me?"

"Our solution impacts many different departments, and no one knows all of the executives within your company better than you, I imagine. I was hoping you would help me figure out the executives in finance, purchasing, and logistics who are responsible for supply-chain planning and execution."

"Our vice president in finance who usually works on supply-chain issues is Norman Fox. Our vice president of purchasing is Penny Johns."

"Patricia, may I say that I got their names directly from you when I call them?"

"Yes, you may."

"My research says that Mary Resch is your vice president of logistics. Is that correct?"

"Yes, it is."

"Thanks so much for your time."

Now Kurt is ready to start making some calls.

Send a Targeted E-Mail or Fax

It can be difficult to get Power on the phone. That's why it's important to soften the path to Power by sending a well-targeted and convincing e-mail or fax to all three of the executives you believe to be Power. Our preference is to send a fax. A fax still ends up front and center on the desk of an executive, particularly if you call their assistant and ask them to place it on top of the desk and not in an in-basket. E-mail filters are powerful, often screening e-mails from unknown sources. And even if your e-mail makes it through the filter, imagine how much face time your e-mail will get given that the average executive gets more than one hundred e-mails each day!

Kurt's fax to Mary Resch at Costline looks like this:

I have done research on Costline and believe you are similar to some of our other customers. Our Global 2000 customers have formed the foundation of an extensive strategic supply-chain management benchmarking study we conducted to determine the specific value we can create for our clients. So, when we tell you that, based on publicly available data, we predict that you're leaving almost $600,000 per month on the table, that's a figure you can believe. We have helped other companies in the same industry as Costline address their critical supply-chain business issues. And your chairman's letter in your annual report indicated that the Costline "Customer first to gain market share" program requires more frequent deliveries to your customers, as well as other key deliverables.

Skeptical? Challenge us. I will be calling you to request a meeting. The purpose of this meeting is to introduce the C3 Value Advantage methodology, further communicate the value we believe you could receive from C3, and compare your company results with others in your line of business and other best-in-class C3 customers. I have sent this same communication to Norman Fox and Penny Johns in order to ensure that I talk with the most appropriate person at Costline.

Our meeting will take approximately 20 minutes. Will you meet with me?

Start a Voice Mail Campaign

In the real world, executives rarely directly answer their phones, so it is important to start an effective voice mail campaign in order to continue to earn the right to speak with an executive. It is important to leave something of value every time you call.

Until you determine specifically who Power is, leave voice mail for all three of the executives you identify through the assistant to the CEO. Call all three on the same day, and then wait at least one week before calling them again. Each time provide the following:

- Who you are and why you're calling—"My name is Kurt Kustner. I'm with C3, and we provide supply-chain solutions."
- Mention your research and that you offer real value—"I have done research on Costline, and based on that research, I believe we can create substantial value."
- Describe the similarities of the prospect to your customers—"My predictive value claim is based on what I have done for my other customers of similar size in your line of business."
- Let them know the names of the other executives you will be calling—"I will be leaving this same message for Norman in finance and Penny in purchasing."
- How to contact you and when you'll be contacting them again—"My phone number is 555-1234, but if I don't hear from you, I'll call back on Friday next week."

Prepare an Executive-Level Brief

While it may not always be necessary, an executive brief that you can send to Power can help you get Power on the phone. The executive brief has two purposes. The first is to serve as a quality mailer to open the door to Power. The second is to serve as a leave-behind after you present to Power, so you don't have to present the same message again before Power sponsors you to verify your value claim. The brief should describe the process you are proposing to engage in with the prospect—essentially, the Zebra Buying Cycle.

The brief should contain the following:

- **Executive summary:** The executive summary describes your process as a fast, high-impact verification of the potential value opportunities created by implementing your solution. Describe your process as one that typically takes one to two business days and concludes with a one- to two-hour presentation summarizing the results. Provide a copy of your Value Waterfall in the summary section, because it communicates your prediction of value for this specific prospect.

- **Introduction:** The introduction explains that the source of your value claim is a benchmarking study you did within your own customer base. Communicate the major areas of benefit—your value drivers—your benchmarking study revealed.

- **Methodology:** The five-step methodology section describes the value-based process. The first step is the research you conduct on each prospect. The second is your prediction of value. The third step is partnering to verify the value. The fourth is a coauthored presentation of the results. And finally, you contract to achieve the results. Be sure to communicate that you recognize you are not done until all the promises that lead to the approval of the project have been met.

- **Impact:** The impact section provides the details on each value driver.

- **Results:** In addition to estimating the value that you can deliver by an investment in your solution, your benchmarking database will also enable you to measure performance versus your peers and other best-in-class performers.

- **Next step:** Meet to discuss this process and how you've helped others of similar size in their industry achieve results.

To see the executive brief that Kurt prepared for Costline, go to the Zebra U site at www.sellingtozebras.com and download the document called Executive Brief.

GETTING A MEETING THE ZEBRA WAY

Think about how many salespeople approach you for appointments. What would happen to your ability to complete your already busy daily schedule if you granted all those appointments? That's the same feeling executives are experiencing as you try to contact them; and that's why you have to hit them with something of interest as soon as you open the conversation.

Follow these steps during your conversation:

1. Inform Power of your research and communicate the pain points you uncovered. Confirm the existence of these pain points.

2. Confirm that Power cares about these pain point business issues and wants to address them now or soon.

3. Link the pain points to what you've done for other customers just like this prospect.

4. Present the prediction of value. (Use those great financials the value model produced for you!)

5. Verify that the amount of incremental value you can create is enough to be worth it to Power to spend twenty minutes discussing it with you. If it isn't, get a referral to someone in the organization, perhaps in a different department or at a different level, who would be interested. (Is this a contradiction? Do you feel we might be suggesting you settle for an appointment with non-Power? No! Read the wake-up call below for an explanation.)

6. Close for a twenty-minute appointment.

 WAKE-UP CALL

Executives at large companies really might not have time for solutions that generate less than $10 million in value over three years. As a rule of thumb, C-level executives—CFOs, COOs, CEOs—will care about solutions that generate enough financial benefit to impact their earnings per share (EPS) by at least $0.01 per year. To put this into perspective, Hewlett-Packard, with annual revenues of more than $100 billion, needs to generate $27 million per year in additional profit to contribute an additional $.01 to shareholder equity. So, for HP's CEO to care about your solution, you would need to create about $81 million over a three-year period ($27 million x 3) in value to get interest. That being said, someone at HP does care about $10 million in bottom-line savings. You just need to ask to be directed to that person.

In trying to attract Power's interest, you may be tempted to hit him with your value proposition right out of the gate. You've developed an amazing prediction of value, and you have your handy Value Waterfall ready to go. This value is meaningless and empty, however, if you haven't first established a dialogue about Power's pain points. Treating specific business issues is what creates real value. When you determine that Power has the same business issues you have solved for other customers, you can communicate a prediction of value and ask for an appointment. Based on your research, you *believe* that Power in your prospect has the same pain points that your solution generally addresses. But what if they don't agree? Then your solution is valueless to them, right? Or what if they don't intend to address those particular pain points anytime soon because of other priorities? That's why this step-by-step information process is so important. You can't assume Power will just connect the dots on his own and propel the relationship to the next step for you. Let's simplify the issue like this:

 **WAKE-UP CALL**

Pain points = Value

Pain points confirmed by Power = Value

Power's desire to address the pain points = Value

No pain points = No value

No pain points confirmed by Power = No value

No desire to address the pain points = No value

Talking to Power: Give Her What She Needs

The six steps we just described are designed to get you what you need in order to continue in the Zebra Buying Cycle. Following those steps will give Power what she needs to agree to a meeting—confirmed potential value. But Power is going to have some questions during the call that you need to be prepared to answer. To help you prepare for these types of calls and execute them effectively, we recommend you develop a call script. To see a sample call script you can pull from, go to the Zebra U site at www.sellingtozebras.com.

In your call script, you should address the following points:

- WHY you are contacting her: your justification for contacting Power, the specific pain points, and your solution
- WHAT you do for companies like the prospect company
- WHY you aren't speaking with a lower-level person in a specific department: further justification for contacting Power
- WHAT is in it for her—hard evidence of value you have generated in the past as a result of solving those same business issues for other clients of similar size in similar industries. Be prepared with the names of these specific, relevant customers in your installed base where you have created this value.
- WHO else you are calling on within her company. There may be multiple points of Power, and it's important to attempt to penetrate the prospect further by communicating with all of them, leveraging that effort, and creating competition so you can get an appointment.
- WHAT it will cost her—just twenty minutes of her time to meet with you
- HOW you would like to set up a meeting

This all may sound simple and intuitive on paper, but as any salesperson knows, once you are on the phone with a prospect, things never seem to flow exactly according to the plan you've laid out. That's why it's so important to go in prepared. As you begin to use this technique, be sure to keep notes on new questions or objections you face so that you can develop appropriate answers and be even more prepared the next time.

Kurt finally has Power at Costline on the phone in the form of Norman Fox. Kurt knew this day would come, so he spent time preparing a call script. He plans to leverage the following key points:

- He got Norman's name from Patricia Jones, assistant to Norman's boss's boss.
- He's pursuing two other like-level executives.
- His research says operational efficiency is uppermost in the mind of Ernst Cornog, CEO of Costline Food Group. It is one of the most important initiatives for Costline this year. It would be fiscally irresponsible of Norman, or the person in charge of the supply chain, not to investigate a savings of just under $600,000 per month.
- He has proof that other similar companies have achieved the level of value creation being discussed.
- He has proof of expertise in the form of a benchmarking survey comparing supply-chain best practices.

"Hello, Mr. Fox, thank you for taking my call. As I mentioned in my messages, C3 provides supply-chain solutions. Last year alone, more than two hundred world-class customers used a supply-chain solution from C3 to bring new financial discipline to more than $850 billion in supply-chain expense."

"How can I help you, Kurt?"

"I've done research on Costline and I believe we can deliver some value. But first I need to ask you a couple of questions. Based on my research, your CEO, Mr. Cornog, has said, 'Costline has reengineered and has increased the flexibility and efficiency of the organization. Costline anticipates pressure on its expense lines this year, so the focus is on controlling overall costs and improving operational efficiency.' Mr. Fox, are you responsible for helping increase supply-chain flexibility and reduce costs this year?"

"I'm involved."

"We know where the supply-chain costs hide. We know where the processes are not rigorous. We live—and thrive—in the world of metrics. Based on publicly available data about Costline, and the most comprehensive strategic supply-chain management benchmarking study of Global 2000 companies ever, we can help you save an additional $600,000 per month. Is an additional $600,000 of unplanned savings per month worth a twenty-minute meeting?"

Norman, "Kurt, did you say in your previous voice mails that you are also contacting Penny in purchasing and Mary in logistics?"

"Yes, I did."

"Why are you chasing all of us?"

"Mr. Fox, I'm looking for the executive who is most directly responsible for the issues I've mentioned so far: increasing flexibility and cost controls. Are you that person?"

"Let's have you talk with Margaret. Margaret is close to our requirements and is managing our drive toward greater supply-chain efficiency. She is putting together an RFP and can make sure you get a copy."

"Mr. Fox, as part of my process I will meet with Margaret, but the C3 customers who have gotten the most value from our solution have executive visibility and direct executive involvement. I would like to share my research, prove I have achieved the additional level of savings we are discussing, and gain your sponsorship. You see, I want to make sure you match my commitment of time and resources in Costline."

"Who else have you met with at Costline?"

"Meeting with you will be my first executive meeting. Are you the most appropriate executive with whom to discuss the potential additional $600,000 per month, and the $0.03 per share EPS impact this savings will generate for Costline shareholders over the next three years?"

"Yes I am. What will this cost?"

"It will cost you twenty minutes of your time."

"Okay, I have my calendar open."

Kurt got his appointment with Power. He leveraged his knowledge of Costline. There are also other reasons Power will grant an appointment. Power doesn't often get an unabridged evaluation of what's happening with competition. Power also doesn't often get to hear an unvarnished and unbiased assessment of what's happening within his own company. If you can provide these insights to the prospect, you'll have additional valuable information that would benefit Power, thus earning you the right to ask for an appointment. For example, imagine you have several customers and prospects in the electronic-games distribution business, and they fit your Zebra. By doing your research on customers and prospects that are all in this same industry, you can simultaneously leverage the common information to all of them at once.

Finally, but even more powerfully, Power is always interested in who else is granting your sales organization an audience. In other words, every connection you have to Power within your customer base and your prospect base can be leveraged into additional appointments with others in positions of Power. By leveraging your past success, you create a level of interest and spur curiosity. They will talk to you to find out with whom you have also been working and talking to and how those customers and prospects are using (or planning to use) your solution. This is how you leverage past success into future success.

This process of getting Power to agree to a meeting is fairly simple, but it requires a shift in thinking for many salespeople who are more comfortable talking about products and features. For this reason, you might want to try role-playing the telephone and meeting techniques with your manager or some other trusted party who would be willing to help you. Role-playing can be an effective learning tool.

You may want to start using these techniques in the real world by approaching a few of your existing customers almost as if they are new prospects. This will create a strong framework for when you call on a new prospect. You will have perfected your technique with accounts where your phone calls should be received at least slightly more warmly than with a new prospect. Plus, when you are done, you will have quotes from existing customers to use, and therefore considerably more confidence when you call prospects. There is just no substitute for the zeal and energy true belief creates. And practice is the only way to obtain this level of confidence.

OK, you've obtained your meeting with Power using the techniques we've outlined. Time to call it a day and celebrate, right? Wrong! Keep pushing ahead. Let's figure out what we're going to do in the meeting that we've worked so hard to get. Or maybe, thanks to this newfound strategy, you didn't have to work as hard as you've worked in the past to get a high-level meeting. Regardless, now is the time to identify some ways to move forward to the next step.

ACING THE MEETING

The objective of your meeting with Power is to get Power to sponsor your value-verification process. Partnering with the prospect to verify your value will help confirm that you can create the value you've told Power you can create, the value you're present-ing in the Value Waterfall. In the next chapter, we'll describe that process in detail, but for now it's important to know that it will take one to two business days; it will help you uncover key solu-tion components that will make the value possible; it will involve working with the managers and employees who will be imple-menting your solution; and it will end with a co-presentation to Power. By getting Power to agree to this partnership, you are get-ting him to help you sell your solution. You're involving Power in the buying cycle and creating a mutual investment that will spur him to keep the process moving forward. This is an essential benefit of the Zebra process.

How do you get Power to approve the process? The same way you got Power to meet with you: identify and confirm the busi-ness issues; confirm that Power would like to address the issues; describe how the value you predict can be created; and prove you have created value in the past. Typically, you will use a presentation to give Power everything needed to make a decision to partner with you to verify the value in one twenty-minute meeting. You'll need to communicate two points:

- The mutual COST of the value verification, which is the disruption to Power's business if she decides to take that next step. Any time a prospect dedicates resources to a proj-ect, there is a cost for both the prospect and you. People who are Power need to know that you recognize their invest-ment, just as you would like them to acknowledge yours.
- WHEN Power can expect results.

As when you requested a meeting with Power, you need to provide everything she needs to make a decision at the end of the meeting. Power should know what she needs to complete the process and be able to determine if the amount of value you have produced for others is worth the time it will require to determine if it can be done for the company. If you do a good job presenting this value to Power, and if the prospect is in fact a Zebra, when you ask Power for approval and sponsorship, the answer should be a slam-dunk "yes."

 WAKE-UP CALL

When working with Power at a new prospect, just asking to understand the CAR process can differentiate you from the competition. By recognizing that Power is going to evaluate the decision to invest in your project against other similar and even dissimilar projects, you will demonstrate an understanding of his business interests that goes beyond the normal sales representative.

Now let's take a look at some of the best ways to ensure that you get to hear that favorite little three-letter word. Let's say your solution has been able to generate $18 million worth of verifiable bottom-line value, as well as other less-quantifiable benefits, for several of your customers in a given industry. A good way to end your meeting and position the next step to Power would go something like this: "If the people you trust verify that the predicted $18 million of value is achievable by addressing your business issues, we would expect you to buy our solution. You would owe us nothing for our time, or for the road map deliverable to achieve this value. Can we shake on it?"

This type of approach may feel a little bold to you, and it should. It is bold. But you are a business person, and you are there for a reason. Power loves boldness; he knows and respects why you are there. If the individual you're dealing with doesn't respect this request, you have not identified Power. At this point in the Zebra Buying Process, you aren't asking for a contract. But you shake hands and ask Power to sponsor the next step with the expectation that if and when you do successfully verify the value, you will do business together.

You may be accustomed to doing a demonstration of your product or solution. In the Zebra Buying Cycle, you may still need to do a demonstration, but only when doing so helps your prospect gain understanding and agreement on how you create value. Any demonstrations or simulations you do will need to focus on the value created by addressing Power's pain points.

To get a clear understanding of how the meeting should be conducted, read on!

Kurt is psyched! He has two meetings scheduled with prospects. The first is with Mary Resch of Costline. (Norman Fox cancelled the meeting he had set with Kurt and did not return Kurt's calls. Undeterred, Kurt contacted and secured an appointment with Mary.) Mary is the vice president of logistics and therefore a potential Power candidate at Costline. The second is with Mark Nem. He's feeling a little anxious about his upcoming meeting with Mark because Kurt knows he has a lot to prove, but he realizes the meeting also presents a great opportunity to practice his new approach. At least Mark knows him and likes him.

Because his meeting is a one-on-one in Mary's office, Kurt isn't going to use his computer to present. Instead, he has printed the materials and is going to present using a professional, leather-bound flip-chart tent that he can set on Mary's desk.

A presentation prepared for
Mary Resch
Vice President, Costline Food Group
by C3, Inc.

After the initial greetings, Kurt jumps right in, understanding that he needs to keep the meeting to twenty minutes, as promised. "Ms. Resch, you've confirmed that you're wrestling with the business issues C3 can address. And you seem to be interested in the value we've been able to create for our customers by addressing those issues.

Agenda

- Research
- Business issues
- Prediction of value
- We have done this before
- How we create the value
- Partner to verify the value

"Well, let's say that I'm interested in learning more," Mary replies cautiously.

"As I mentioned on the phone," Kurt continues, "we have researched your business. Our research consisted of a review of your website and other publicly available information. We have come to the conclusion that you are similar to some of our other customers. You have certain key business issues in common, business issues C3 has helped these customers address. By addressing these issues, we've been able to create value for our existing customers, and we think we can create similar value for you. I will show you how and where we've done this before. I'll also provide you with the information you need in order to decide to take the next step. If we address everything I just mentioned, would you consider this to be a successful first meeting?"

"Yes, I think so," Mary agrees.

Costline Business Issues

The chairman's letter in your annual report indicated Costline is implementing an initiative called "Customer first to gain market share." This initiative specifically has led to

- Customers demanding increase in frequency, decrease in size of shipments
- Proliferation of goods coming from China increasing inventory in your supply chain and creating a lack of visibility
- Customers demanding that Costline use radio frequency identification devices

C3

"From our research, we know Costline has a company-wide initiative called 'Customer first to gain market share.' This initiative has created a need to address your customers' demand for an increase in the frequency and a decrease in the size of shipments so they can, in turn, compete with the big-box retailers. You are sourcing more and more nonperishable goods from China, causing an increase in inventory within your supply chain and creating a lack of visibility. And finally, your customers are demanding you tag items with radio frequency identification devices (RFID) to provide better inventory tracking. If we are able to successfully address these issues, as we have done for others—"

"Whom have you talked to in my organization to find out about these issues?" Mary inquires with an impressed look on her face.

Kurt answers, "I took this information from your website and the Hoover's business website, and I did other Internet searches to learn about you and earn the right to meet with you."

"Very good. Thank you," Mary states.

"Are these issues current priorities you intend to resolve? In other words, *is there urgency?*" Kurt questions.

Mary replies without hesitation, "The 'Customer First' initiative is top of mind for all of us at Costline."

"Good," Kurt says. "Then given your answers and what we have done for other customers very similar to Costline, I predict we will be able to generate more than $21 million of value for Costline over the next three years. I'm confident this can be done because we've *done it before* for customers that are similar to Costline in industry, size, and business issues."

Year of Benefit	EBIT	Income After Taxes	EPS Impact
2008/2009	$1,962,125	$1,275,381	N/A
2009/2010	$8,814,309	$5,729,301	N/A
2010/2011	$10,630,504	$6,909,828	N/A
2011/2012	$0	$0	N/A
2012/2013	$0	$0	N/A
TOTALS	**$21,406,938**	**$13,914,509**	**N/A**

Direct & Indirect Savings

Waterfall Ramp-Up	2008/2009	2009/2010	2010/2011
	50%	80%	95%

"What do you mean, you predict you can generate more than $21 million of value for me? That's a pretty bold claim," Mary says, folding her arms.

"Yes, it is. But we *have* done it before. HTK Distribution is one C3 customer that is similar to Costline in size and industry vertical. We were able to generate $17 million in value for HTK over three years. And we have successfully addressed these business issues and generated this level of value for other, similar customers, such as Web Foods."

We Have Done This Before

"Our efficiency is through the roof and it is because of C3. We experienced a six-month ROI and a three-year EVA of over $17 million."
—James Steelburg, COO, HTK Distribution, Inc.

"We have experienced such a dramatic reduction in our supply chain cycle time that we refer to points in time as B-C3 and A-C3 (Before C3 and After C3).
—Diedra Web, Vice President of Supply Chain Planning, Web Foods, Inc.

"And how do you create this value?" Mary asks, not realizing she is playing into the flow of the presentation.

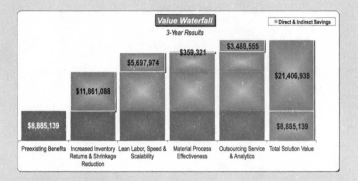

"I'm glad you asked," Kurt says appreciatively. "This is a graphical representation of value created by the functional components of our solution. Our conservative prediction of value for Costline is $21 million. In this graphic, we have 'pillarized' our value, so to speak. For example, starting from the left with our second pillar, our customers say that we increase inventory turns, thus reducing inventory and the shrinkage of inventory. This is one of our more basic solution benefits put into actual quantifiable results others have achieved, and therefore what you could expect as well. We increase inventory turns beyond what any of our competitors have been able to accomplish to date.

"Labor is our next pillar of value. Support for lean labor techniques and the associated speed and flexibility that come from the deployment of our supply-chain techniques are direct benefits of our solution.

"As we move all the way to the right, you'll see that we can offer your business a completely outsourced solution, in which case we take over all the ongoing operational aspects of the C3-provided solution. And when we do so, we use our analytics software to ensure that uptime targets are achieved and cost is reduced. Is how we drive value starting to become clearer?" Kurt asks.

"Yes, I'm starting to understand. What is that first pillar—the one titled Preexisting Benefits?" Mary asks.

"We realize that companies such as yours almost always have partial solutions in place to deal with the business issues we address. Therefore some of the possible benefit has already been realized. The Preexisting Benefits pillar separates the already potentially realized benefit from the benefit that we project is possible with our solution. We will need to verify this, but from our preliminary research, we concluded you already have systems in place that will help you realize over the next three years as much as $8.8 million of the value that is possible with our solution. We calculate preexisting benefits so we don't *overstate* the value we would be *responsible* for creating for Costline."

Mary sits quietly, reflecting on what has just been presented. With a hand on her chin she replies, "This is almost a little offensive. You make me feel as though my people and I should already be doing more of this, and therefore receiving more of this $21 million potential benefit."

"Oh," Kurt says, as Mary's comment has caught him off guard. "That's not my intent at all." After a bit of embarrassing silence, Kurt rallies. "You see, some of the components of our solution were not previously available, so you and others could not have been expected to achieve this type of positive result. The combined use of the pieces of our solution creates a unique synergy also not previously available, and therefore the results were not previously achievable."

"Thanks for letting me off the hook," Mary says, satisfied—at least for the moment. "So, in other words, your solution is so new,

I couldn't have achieved these results before, and I can't achieve them now by working with a different vendor?"

Kurt continues, "Not until now. And no, no one does what C3 does quite the way we do it. Do you want to give us a chance to convince you and the people you trust that we can drive this level of value for your business?"

Next Step: Partner to Verify Value

- Costline's Commitment
    - Access to key personnel in operations, finance, and supply chain
    - Twenty to thirty man-hours over two business days
- Value Verification
    - Identify current state, future state, and value improvements
    - Your team assesses value claim
- Time Frame—Verification process completed and findings presented in three weeks
- Result—Road map for achieving value
- Cost

"Maybe. Tell me what that would involve."

"The next logical step is to partner to verify our prediction of value. To do this, we use a collateralized, repeatable process. We need only twenty to thirty man-hours of your people's time over a two-day period. We have a tight agenda that allows us to gather the information we need from your own trusted process owners and to execute the process with precision to verify our value. When we're done, we'll present to you the value your people have verified and will provide a presentation that serves as a road map for achieving that value. If we go forward with this partnering step, I would be back in your office in about three weeks," Kurt says, "to present the results and a proposal. At that time I would provide all the information you need to make a decision regarding doing business with C3."

Looking Mary in the eye, Kurt continues. "Now, I'm a businessperson, and as such my ultimate objective is to do business. So, I would like to enter into a simple agreement. If we successfully identify, and your people agree we can achieve, at least the $21 million we predict over three years—I will expect you to move forward and do business with C3. If we can't verify, we go away."

"We do have other initiatives under way to address these issues," Mary shares. "Although I like your approach, I can't guarantee you'll have the business when you're finished, even if you can get my people to agree it's possible. However, if you and your people continue to conduct business in such an organized and professional fashion as you have demonstrated today, your company will have an excellent shot at a piece of business with Costline."

"That's fair," Kurt replies. "I'll take the risk and invest my staff's time to convince you of what's possible. Are you ready to start identifying the people who will fill the operations, finance, and supply-chain roles on the verification team?"

Mary takes a moment to consider the proposal, flipping through the printed slides one more time. "Okay, yes," she states. "Tell me the type of information you'll need and I'll identify contacts in our organization and make sure you're introduced."

"Wonderful," Kurt says, pulling out his pad of paper in order to take notes. *Impossible quota, you've met your match!* he shouts in his head, then asks one more question. "Can you also tell me the name of the person I could work with to understand the capital appropriation request process used at Costline to evaluate alternative expenditures of capital?"

With a look of respect, Mary replies, "We call it CE—capital expenditures—but yes I can."

After Kurt's successful meeting with Mary, and because of his research preparation, he delivers an equally compelling presentation to Mark Nem . . . but the sailing is not as smooth.

Kurt knows Mark is more skeptical than a new prospect. After all, there have been problems between C3 and Nem's in the past, and C3 has definitely not done its part to force the success of past agreements. Mark's people want to work with another supplier. To address this issue, Kurt adds two slides to his arsenal. The first is an honest assessment of C3's past sins. Just after getting Mark's confirmation of the pain points, Kurt addresses the past problems at Nem's: "We didn't propose enough support, education, or partner management with our first implementation. I'm here to make that right."

The second new slide is an analysis of the value that Nem's has and could have achieved with the current C3 solution they have in place, using the achieved-value radar diagram. Kurt flips to it and says, "For this reason and others, you haven't gotten all of the value you should be getting from the C3 solution you already own. In fact, this is how you compare to some of our best-in-class customers."

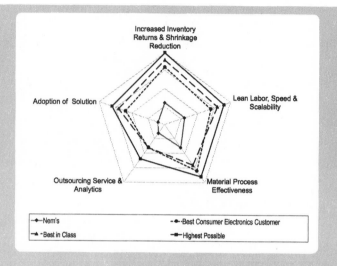

Tracing the innermost line of the graphic, Kurt explains: "Mark, I have talked with our people. What this line shows is that Nem's is at about a 6 out of a possible score of 18, or is receiving about 33 percent of the benefit you could hope to achieve with lean labor and the associated speed and scalability of lean. The dotted line with circles shows where our best consumer-products company rates on this same metric. And the line with triangles shows where our best-in-class customer rates. The line with the square points shows the highest possible scores. As you can see, Nem's is pretty far from those results. I don't want to offend you, but not all the issues associated with poor value are ours alone. Through policy and process changes, there is more value that Nem's could get from the supply-chain solution you previously purchased from us."

Mark doesn't say anything so Kurt continues. "On the phone I mentioned we had supply-chain answers to questions that haven't been asked by the recent Nem's RFP. For example, what is your supply-chain bottleneck—the weakest, slowest link in your supply chain? Do you subordinate the schedules in front of that weak link and behind it, smoothing your entire supply chain and reducing the buildup of inventory?"

"You know we don't, Kurt," Mark responds, a little annoyed. "Why haven't you helped us do that in the past?"

"Both our companies have behaved in a less-than-optimal way. I've owned our issues, and I'm here to talk about a way to fix them. There are also issues on the Nem's side that we haven't addressed with you. Together we can fix both, and extract the additional untapped value. Interested?"

"I guess I should be," Mark says hesitantly.

Kurt proceeds to share the Value Waterfall he had generated for Nem's and then presses to move to the next step. "Make me prove this to you and your people," he challenges.

"Not just yet," Mark responds, obviously in thought. Silence fills the room while Mark continues to ponder Kurt's question. "You're obviously taking a different approach than you took before, and I'm inclined to make you prove your claim. But how are you going to repair the relationship you have with our project manager?"

"Our goal is to make her look good," Kurt responds, obviously prepared for the question. He then proceeds to explain how he has set the ramp-up percentages conservatively so that C3 claims only a percentage of the total benefit possible in the early implementation stages. "This technique allows us to provide plenty of time to ensure absorption of change and all but guarantees we have remained conservative in our value projections. It's all part of our new process."

"Oh, I like that. That would have helped us the first time we did business with you, wouldn't it?" Mark asks with a pointed look at Kurt. "Okay, let's do it. I'll give you a chance to prove all of this."

Kurt is elated. Even with prior problematic customer relationships, the new approach is working.

WAKE-UP CALL .

This approach to the meeting with Power works because

- It's predictive—the model predicts the value generated by the solution

- It addresses Power's pain points—it ties pain points to the prediction of value

- The salesperson becomes the messenger—"We have done this before, and this is the value customers have achieved"

- It frames disruption to the business—it can verify value in two days with twenty to thirty man-hours of the prospect's time

- It frames chronology—the assessment will take three weeks, start to finish

- It verifies value of opportunity—with Power's trusted process owners

- It clearly communicates what is deliverable—it presents a roadmap to create value

- It requests a decision in the first meeting—"Will you partner to verify this value?"

You've done it! You've gotten through the hardest part of the process. You've identified your Zebra, built your model for predicting value, found an appropriate prospect, and gotten him to agree to sponsor your efforts to prove the value you can create. The next step, while new, is easy compared to what you've accomplished so far. Get ready to learn how to prove your value and close your Zebra.

CHAPTER 7

PARTNER TO VERIFY YOUR VALUE

THE VALUE VERIFICATION IS ONE OF THE most exciting parts of the Zebra Buying Cycle. It gets you inside a company to discover exactly what your products can do for the prospect. This is your best selling time!

Are you typically required to demonstrate your solution as part of your sales process? If you are, then you probably have participated in the dreaded show-up-and-throw-up demonstration. Demo Don or Dolly demonstrates all the whiz-bang features and functions of the solution. Prospects sit with their notes from their RFP and score the various functional components. If, in their perception, the way you address a feature or function satisfies a need, they check it off or even score it for comparison against your competition. When the demo is finished, a nameless, faceless person will add up the scores and make a decision. That person might even have the help of a consultant, who is almost always predisposed to one company's solution. Scores only matter if they support the predisposition. In a truly objective RFP process—which only happens when the evaluation is run by saints or liars—two vendors rise to the surface. Then the evaluation team tosses the two options over the wall to procurement. Procurement works its magic, positioning the vendors against each other so that a good deal eventually emerges. Your solution, to the best of the evaluation team's ability, has been commoditized. You've been reduced to your component parts of value equal to and no greater than the competition, and now procurement can beat the stuffing out of you.

Value verification avoids this ordeal by providing confirmation of two things for the prospect: Power's pain points exist and align with your solution; and you can create the value you claim to generate by addressing these pain points. Confirmation of these two points is crucial to customer satisfaction.

The steps of the value verification are as follows:

- Power identifies the team of people you'll work with during the value verification.
- Power and the verification team complete surveys (the same survey you sent to the Zebras in your customer base) to help you structure the process and estimate the value you used to build your value model.
- You work with Power's team for two days to gather the information necessary to verify your value.
- You adjust your value model based on the information you've gathered and create a road map presentation that describes how the value will be achieved.
- You and Power's team present the findings to Power.

The greatest sales benefit of the value verification process is the partnership you create with Power and with trusted members of management in support of your solution, which allows you to design a solution with *all* of the components necessary to ensure that the prospect actually achieves the promised value. When you sell this way, you don't have to fight to include the proper education, integration, project management, consulting, partner management, or any other elements needed to deliver the value. They aren't seen as extras, they're expected! Instead of getting beaten down at the end of a sales cycle because your price is too high, acquiescing and removing solution components you know are necessary for success, it's your responsibility to include *everything* you will need to achieve the value you've verified. And the people responsible for the long-term success of the project—those who handle the implementation—will have everything they need to be successful and create a happy customer your company can use as a reference. The value verification is critical to the Force Success philosophy.

This is why the value verification is so compelling for salespeople and their prospects. Since you have been religiously following our recommendations so far, you have set the solution investment portion of your model high; built your model using the low end of all value-claim ranges from customer surveys; and reduced your solution to conservative, slow-adoption levels by setting low ramp-up percentages. These actions should make verifying your value a fairly easy process.

THE TEAM PLAYERS

To achieve everything you need to achieve during the value verification, you must have the right team in place. From your company, bring your sales team, the people who are responsible for determining the necessary components of the product or solution (for less-complex solutions or products, that might be *just you*), and the people who will be responsible for the implementation. You will work with the solution designers to conduct the process, but the implementation team should be involved in the creation of the final proposal. This provides an opportunity to get them excited about it on a personal level and will help you identify any potential implementation issues right at the beginning so that they can be addressed in your proposal.

 WAKE-UP CALL

In traditional sales cycles, the implementation team typically meets the customer for the first time after the project has been sold. This creates a situation in which, after the sales process is complete and implementation begins, some aspects of the sales process have to begin again. This "do over" can create the seeds of project difficulties or even failure. As time goes on and implementation proceeds, details that weren't anticipated have to be added to project plans. Suddenly the priorities established by sales and the prospect start to shift. Complex solution implementations start to bog down as strong end users with competing agendas start to influence the implementation of the project.

In the Zebra Buying Cycle, the value verification helps sales set clear goals for the implementation of the solution. The goals are clear because they are quantifiable and established by the prospect (Power and management), the sales team, and the implementation team. Because of the value verification, it's much easier to keep everyone focused and staying the course during implementation.

The prospect's team should include the people who will be involved in implementing, managing, and using your product or solution. These are the members of management that Power has identified who will help you uncover the process improvements and solution components that, if implemented, will drive the value possible with your solution. For example, if one of your value drivers is reduction in labor, you'll likely work with the manager who is responsible for the specific process your solution addresses. That person will review the before-and-after effort required to perform the tasks in order to verify that the labor reduction value you claim is possible can actually happen.

In addition to the manager who is responsible for the budget for a given process, area, or department, someone from the prospect's finance department should be involved in all meetings. Finance knows how the prospect's capital appropriation process works. Therefore, they can help by determining which savings claims will be included in the CAR document. Finance will also know how the company likes to look at ROI data as it makes capital decisions. Some companies look at the ROI and NPV. Others will look at the ROI, payback period, and IRR. Still others will require every calculation your model automatically generates. This information will help you structure your final presentation to Power on the results of the value verification.

If you are adding additional discipline or control to a given area, you should have representatives of that area involved. For example, if, like C3, your solution allows you to add procurement discipline to a purchasing process, a manager from the procurement team should be assigned to help with the value verification.

One of our customers offers software that helps its Fortune 2000 customers plan and source meetings more efficiently and effectively. They are able to aggregate meeting expenditures for lodging, air travel, rental cars, and food and beverages for their clients. Consequently, their clients are able to leverage their purchasing power to get better deals. Therefore, the appropriate team to assemble for value verifications would include the prospect's meeting managers, who own the process; finance managers, who understand the ins and outs of the internal CAR process; and procurement managers, because a key component of the value will be derived from implementing procurement negotiating techniques and discipline to meeting management expenditures.

THE SURVEY

The same survey used to determine the value you've created in your existing customer base will be used to establish your partnership with new prospects. That survey is given to Power to help her identify who is best equipped to answer your survey questions. When Power identifies the members of the value verification team, send the survey to each of those people.

Your survey will include only those questions that will help you uncover the big savings areas. Don't get too nitty-gritty. If you know answers to any of the questions based on your specific knowledge of the account or the industry (as you should), fill in those answers on the surveys you distribute. The prospect's survey participants can use your numbers as a gauge of reasonableness to assess the validity of their answers. You will establish trust and confidence when you help the team members help themselves.

When the surveys are in hand, set up phone calls with the participants to address their questions so they are prepared for your visit. When you meet face to face you will help them complete the survey accurately, but this pre-verification step will help break the ice and will begin to establish you as the expert. Make the process as painless and efficient as possible. If you know the answer to questions better than the prospect, then answer them, and demonstrate that expertise.

VERIFYING YOUR VALUE

Depending on the complexity of your solution, the value verification occurs over one or two days and requires between five and thirty man-hours of the prospect's time. You'll work with a predetermined schedule that identifies what will happen, when, and with which team members. We've presented a sample agenda from Kurt's value verification with Costline.

The two-day partnering exercise is launched the morning of the first day by your Power-level sponsor. Power will discuss the objective of the exercise, state the value that has prompted her to support the effort, and discuss desired outcomes. Power's immediate involvement will serve to diffuse any opposition to your presence. Process owners can be territorial. For example, meeting managers at our clients' prospect companies are often comfortable with the status quo of their positions. They aren't necessarily interested in learning a new tool, new ways of doing business, or applying new discipline to their processes, even if such change could generate millions of dollars of savings. Their cooperation is necessary and assured when Power, whether he is vice president of finance or procurement or the COO, launches the value verification, demonstrating a keen desire to achieve whatever level of benefit might be possible.

WAKE-UP CALL

The factor that can most easily derail a value verification is a process owner who refuses to verify the value claims. This is why Power's involvement—during the launch meeting, at the beginning of day two, and at the end of the process—is so important. Without true sponsorship from the executive, the results may not happen, so it's best to find out now if there is a true commitment from Power. Projects succeed when they have executive sponsorship, commitment, and ongoing follow-up, and when they are monitored at the executive level.

After Power has launched the meeting, you will run through the original presentation you made to Power and review the two-day agenda. Individual meetings are then conducted with the process owners and any other subject matter experts who are needed, as well as with a representative from finance. You begin by reviewing and completing the surveys. You and your experts should have enough knowledge to determine whether some answers are outliers and may be misleading. This is where your expertise starts to help you.

Getting to Verification

To develop an accurate estimate of the value you can create for your prospect, you have to discuss each of the business issues highlighted in your Value Waterfall (your value drivers) with the owners of those business issues. This will help you identify when an issue is somehow addressed by other existing solutions and discuss or even demonstrate the new, improved ability to address the issue. This is how the value generated with your proposed improvements is verified.

Value Verification Agenda

C3 Participants

> Kurt Kustner, Vice President of Operations
>
> Dave Fowl, Manager of Presales Consultants

Costline Participants

> Mary Resch, Vice President, Logistics
>
> Cynthia Hart, Senior Manager, Procurement
>
> Bob Wright, Finance
>
> Ned Kine, Warehouse Manager

Day 1 Agenda

8:00 to 8:30: Overview of value verification process and final deliverables

> Pre-meeting requirements: Gather data on supply-chain planning expenditures, process, and policies (catalyst—C3 benchmark survey sent to prospect)
>
> Participants: All members of both teams
>
> Meeting launched by Mary Resch, executive sponsor
>
> Present Value Waterfall and explain verification process, Kurt of C3

8:30 to 10:00: Review survey (completed by C3 and Costline with known and estimated data)

> Pre-meeting requirements: Familiarity with C3 benchmark survey
>
> Participants: Supply-chain management, procurement, finance
>
> *Conduct C3 benchmark survey. Score results.*
>
> *Gather data and evidence of current situation as they relate to each value driver line item, establish and get agreement on desired best practice and value of best-practice solution component (demonstrate solution, where necessary, to explain and get agreement on value and understanding of best-practice recommendations).*
>
> *Participants leave meeting to gather or verify information wherever needed.*

10:00 to 10:15—*Break*

10:15 to 11:30: Review survey continued

Pre-meeting requirements: C3 Supply-chain planning process maturity benchmark

Participants: Supply chain, finance

Continue to conduct C3 benchmark survey. Score results.

Continue to gather data and evidence of current situation as it relates to each detail value driver line item, establish and get agreement on desired best practice and value of best-practice solution component (demonstrate solution, where necessary, to explain and get agreement of value and understanding of best-practice recommendations).

Participants leave meeting as necessary to gather or verify information.

11:30 to 1:00—Lunch

1:00 to 3:00: Review survey continued

Pre-meeting requirements: C3 Supply-chain process maturity benchmark

Participants: Procurement, finance

Continue to conduct C3 benchmark survey. Score results.

Continue to gather data and evidence of current situation as it relates to each value driver line item, establish and get agreement on desired best practice and value of best-practice solution component (demonstrate solution, where necessary, to explain and get agreement of value and understanding of best-practice recommendations).

Participants leave meeting as necessary to gather or verify information wherever possible.

3:00 to 3:15—Break

3:15 to 5:00: Begin creation of value verification coauthored presentation

Participants: Supply chain, procurement, finance

Review the value verification template presentation and fill in the current state, future state, best-practice recommendations, and subsequent verified value.

Evening: C3 team enters survey data in the model and completes Value Waterfall with verified data.

C3 value verification team finishes a draft of a "Value Verification Road Map Presentation," including current state, future state, best-practice recommendations, and subsequent value.

Day 2 Agenda
8:00 to 8:30: Value verification status check
      Pre-meeting requirements: None
      Participants: Executive sponsor
      Review any issues.

8:30 to 10:00: Building the verified value presentation
      Participants: Supply chain, procurement, finance
      Review current state, future state, best-practice recommendations, and resulting value to get confirmation, buy-in. Review, adjust, coauthor "Value Verification Road Map Presentation."

10:00 to 10:15—Break

10:15 to 12:00: Review of financial metrics produced by the model
      Participants: Supply chain, procurement, finance

      Review outputs from Value Waterfall model (PowerPoint slides with cut-and-paste financial data; waterfall, financial evaluation of alternative uses of capital, direct and indirect savings, payback period graph)

12:00 to 1:30—Lunch

1:30 to 4:30: Technical interviews
      Pre-meeting requirements: C3 technical specs for presentation
      Participants: Supply chain, engineers
        General information
- Discussion of C3 solution requirements
- Integration requirements
- Third-party information systems requirements

4:30 to 5:00: Recap and plan next step
      Participants: Executive sponsor
      Set date for final presentation

With the Zebra Buying Cycle, demonstrations are very different. Each demonstration is process specific, with the objective of showing how the new process eliminates the pain and problems associated with the old process. The demonstration lasts only as long as it takes to get agreement from the prospect of the value created.

A discovery text document describing each value driver from the model is used to guide and partner Power's trusted people to verify the value. The text document mirrors your value model. The document has the same value driver section as your model. It also has the comments on each of the value drivers explaining the low-end and high-end range of value that customers reported they received—just like we described in chapter 5. After you have reviewed the prospect's current process and demonstrated how the new solution simplifies that process, you present the low end and the best-practice high end of the savings range. The final step is to get the client to agree that at least the lowest level of savings is possible.

As part of the verification process, you'll also need to get the prospect team members to agree on other key components of your value model, such as the ramp-up time frame and level of adoption. If you followed our advice in chapter 5 and set your initial estimates very conservatively, you'll be in a strong position. Once the process owners see that your solution makes their jobs easier, you'll be able to ask if they feel it's reasonable to use adoption percentages that are slightly higher than in your original value prediction. So, if you used 40 percent for the first year, maybe they'll agree to 50 percent in the first year, and so on. With this approach, even if you don't get agreement and verification of all of the individual line items associated with each value driver verified, you will still have increased the verified total value you will be able to present back to Power. And that's the best position to be in.

That said, the number one reason Power-level executives might not approve a cost-justified proposal has nothing to do with your solution. They believe your solution works. They believe your customers have been successful. They also don't doubt that your people are capable of delivering. The number one reason Power is nervous and won't approve an ROI-positive project is that he doesn't believe his own people can be successful and deliver the advertised results. Therefore, as you partner to verify the value, you and your team are assessing the management process owners to gauge the level of help they'll need and the amount of time necessary to be successful. If necessary, this may mean slowing the implementation by lowering the percentages in the ramp-up portion of the model. Lowering the ramp-up will slow the expected financial benefits and overall three-year value, but it will raise the likelihood of success. If you lower the ramp-up and in your final presentation to Power deliver a Value Waterfall less than what was presented in your first meeting, you'll do so knowing that what is being proposed is what will be delivered. Power can sense strength. You will be presenting from strength, and your chance of a "yes" will still be strong because you will have addressed Power's number one, often unvoiced, concern.

 WAKE-UP CALL

Only look for the big pieces of value. Don't go any deeper than the components of your value drivers. Any more detail than that will bog the process down. Demonstrate your subject matter expertise by streamlining the process; don't require the prospect team member to describe in great detail every aspect of their business. With the Zebra way, less is more.

Kurt knows that the big pieces of value generation for his company are increases in inventory turns, reduction of labor spent moving goods, process improvements that reduce cycle time, and better visibility and instantaneously available information. In the supply-chain space, Kurt and his team know where the C3 process will eliminate steps. They know that the savings hide in places like too many steps that involve paperwork or handling goods. Moving goods over and over increases supply-chain time and increases the risk of loss or damage. The elimination of steps saves time and labor and reduces shrinkage of inventory due to damage. And his customer survey results prove C3 creates these savings!

Kurt is meeting with Costline's warehouse manager, Ned Kine. He's trying to get to an agreement of the value that C3 can create for Ned's department by reducing labor costs. "Our customers have verified that they now can move materials in the warehouse with less," Kurt tells Ned. "The estimated savings our customers report due to fewer FTEs required to generate paperwork and move the materials is a minimum of 0.15 percent and a best-practice maximum of 0.30 percent of total supply-chain expenditure. We have demonstrated all the ways we simplify and automate this process. Would you prefer we use the minimum, or are you more bullish about your ability to drive a higher level of savings?"

When you're trying to get to verification, it's imperative you believe that your solution and the value you're claiming are possible. Do not—repeat, DO NOT—offer to cut your savings in half. An oft-used but weak technique is to present ROI benefits that others have achieved and then say something like, "Even if I cut these savings in half, they're still amazing. Would you feel more comfortable if I cut these savings in half?" You have to have the courage of your convictions, already knowing you have been conservative in your savings projections. If you know that the absolute minimum any of your customers achieved was a reduction of 0.15 percent of hourly payroll as a result of using your solution, don't agree to a lower figure. It's not going to help you close the sale with Power, who will sense you don't believe your own value claims.

THE NEW VALUE PREDICTION AND THE ROAD MAP TO SUCCESS

The goal of all of this work is to come to an agreement on the level of savings possible for each value driver. You will have taken notes on your value discussions, including notes on the processes the prospect team members described and how your solution can improve them. And you'll have your final numbers in hand. Now, the night after your first day of value verification meetings, you can plug the quantities back into your model in the privacy of your office or your hotel room. And voilà: You've got a new, verified Value Waterfall—and all of the other financials and graphics you'll need to present the results of the value verification to Power and justify the decision to buy from you!

Kurt is working through the data he gathered from the value verification with Costline. He and his solution engineers showed the Costline process owners how the material "put-away" information could be automatically generated as a result of the C3 implementation. The warehouse manager agreed that after a three-month implementation, more than 50 percent of all Costline products could easily be controlled by the new system in the first year. Second-year levels were agreed at 80 percent, and he was actually pleased to approve a third-year expectation of 95 percent, feeling that allowed for a 5 percent margin of error because the expectation was never to get 100 percent material compliance with the new C3 system. (It might be possible to achieve 100 percent, but again, Kurt's claim is a more conservative 95 percent.)

Kurt's original prediction of value was set with an expected implementation time of four months and a ramp-up of 40 percent the first year, 75 percent the second year, and 90 percent the third year. These parameters produced benefits of an ROI of 1,189 percent over three years, an NPV of $16.8 million, an EVA of $13.4 million, an IRR of 351 percent, a payback period of eight months, and a monthly cost of indecision of just under $600,000.

Direct & Indirect Savings	
ROI of this project over 3 years is:	1189%
NPV of this project over 3 years is:	$16,827,409
EVA of this project over 3 years is:	$13,482,509
IRR of this project over 3 years is:	351%
Payback Period of this project is:	8 Months
Monthly cost of indecision is:	$594,637

Waterfall Ramp-Up	2008/2009	2009/2010	2010/2011
	40%	75%	90%

When Kurt enters the newly verified ramp-up and adoption expectations into the model, he is delighted by the results!

All of the financial metrics are more robust than they were in his original estimate. The ROI went from 1,189 percent to 1,301 percent, the NPV is now more than $18.5 million, the EVA is now more than $14.7 million, the IRR is now 402 percent, and the monthly cost of indecision is $650,000! Kurt knows he is in a strong position for his final presentation to Mary Resch.

Direct & Indirect Savings	
ROI of this project over 3 years is:	1301%
NPV of this project over 3 years is:	$18,516,399
EVA of this project over 3 years is:	$14,794,206
IRR of this project over 3 years is:	402%
Payback Period of this project is:	7 Months
Monthly cost of indecision is:	$650,693

Waterfall Ramp-Up	2008/2009	2009/2010	2010/2011
	50%	80%	95%

Once you've adjusted your prediction of value, you'll build your value road map, which is the final presentation you will make to Power. The road map presentation describes the before-and-after picture of each process associated with each value driver. Each step that produces errors or requires lots of time and money is noted. The new process, agreed to by Power's process managers, highlights the elimination of steps, errors, and time, and the other ways you drive value have been verified and documented. The presentation also includes pictures or descriptions of your solution that help to demonstrate how you eliminate the steps, errors, and time. A sample of the value verification presentation can be found on our website at www.sellingtozebras.com. The second day of partnering to verify your value is spent reviewing, adjusting, and coauthoring the template presentation you created the previous night.

In planning the project timeline, note that the value verification exercise takes only two days, but the final results typically are not ready for two to three weeks. During this period there are additional meetings to address any specific issues that were identified as part of the initial value verification, allowing the prospect to check references or do other follow-up tasks, such as review and comment upon your value verification road map presentation, so the end result is a coauthored presentation for the final meeting with Power.

THE PRESENTATION TO POWER

Once you've completed the value verification, you're ready to return to Power to present your results. You should schedule a two-hour meeting with Power and the value verification team. You'll need plenty of time to present findings on each of the business issues or value drivers and address any questions Power has. During the meeting you'll discuss

- before-and-after processes
- the value you were able to verify
- your solution, through the road map that demonstrates how your solution eliminates steps, reduces errors, and saves time and money
- the financial justification for the project
- a commitment from Power to do business

The presentation you coauthor with the prospect's value verification team defines the present state, the future desired state, and your solution components, which when implemented create the verified value. Lucky for you, the model you've been using throughout the process automatically creates the financial data and the graphics you'll need to make the business case for purchasing your solution. Power will respect that you have included the financials she will need in order to make a decision. The most powerful in terms of closing the sale will be the monthly cost of prospect indecision (see the bottom of the figure on page 192). If people in Power have the pain points you're addressing and believe their own people's numbers, this really is what they are losing every month without your solution! Here are some of the graphics the model auto generates for you, payback period graph, financial summary, financial detail, solution investment, and of course the Value Waterfall.

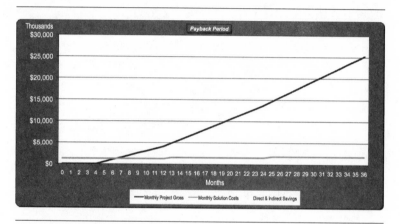

Final Payback Period Graph

3-Year Results -- Direct & Indirect Savings	
EBIT Impact	$23.42M
P&L Impact	$15.23M
Payback Period	7 Months
Cost of Indecision	$650,693 per month

Financial Summary

Year of Benefit	EBIT	Income After Taxes	EPS Impact	
2008/2009	$2,769,322	$1,800,060		N/A
2009/2010	$9,419,707	$6,122,810		N/A
2010/2011	$11,235,902	$7,303,337		N/A
2011/2012	$0	$0		N/A
2012/2013	$0	$0		N/A
TOTALS	$23,424,932	$15,226,206		N/A
Direct & Indirect Savings				

Financial Detail

To conclude your presentation, you will present a Value Waterfall that has now been verified, as well as your Force Success proposal. That proposal allows you to look Power in the eye and state that you have everything in your proposal needed to Force Success—to achieve the value you and her process owners are claiming is possible and to ensure that Power can fulfill the promises she will make to get the project approved. Inclusion of all of these elements earns you the right to ask for the business.

Kurt presents the Costline before-and-after improvements and communicates the verified value associated with each. He then discusses the net value claims after removing the costs of his proposal.

C3 3-Year Solution Investment:	$1,800,000
Enter all cost amounts below in US Dollars $	
Initial Solution Investment Cost	$1,000,000
Costline Food Group Internal Personnel Cost (total for years 1-3)	$200,000
Solution Maintenance (total for years 1-3)	$600,000
Estimated Implementation Time (*in months*)	4.0

"The required solution investment in C3 is the $1.0 million shown here," Kurt says, pointing to the screen. "We recognize that you will have a one-time additional cost equal to about 20 percent of the initial solution investment ($200,000), and the ongoing maintenance of our solution is $600,000 over the next three years.

"The net of all costs, or verified value, of the C3 solution is now $23.4 million [see the Waterfall graph].

"In conclusion, could we discuss the timing to start this implementation, and would you like to review our contract?"

"This has all been very impressive," Mary Resch responds. "I was thinking I might personally need to see a demonstration of your system, though," she says in a tone indicating she is talking more to herself than to anyone in the room. "But maybe not, because your value presentation did a good job of showing me how your solution works and simplifies many of our processes. I would, however, like to walk through the details of your labor-related value one more time."

Kurt is ready for Mary's request, addressing each process that reduces labor, and asking for confirmation from Mary's trusted process owners, who are in the back of the room. Heads nod as he presents the last current process, future process, and confirmed value.

Mary responds, "I feel comfortable with your proposal. I also feel you have more conservatively included everything we will need to actually achieve the value projections. No need for

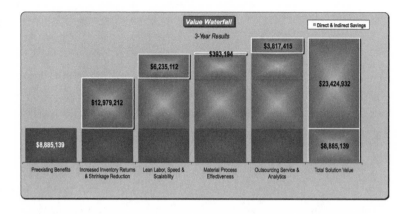

contracts just yet. We first need to complete our internal documentation to get this project approved. The detailed financial analysis will help to streamline that process. We do have one issue, however. Corporate financial policy dictates we bring two viable solutions to our purchasing department before negotiations can commence. We have pieces of other solutions, but no one else has been as thorough or as convincing as C3. You will have to help me present this solution to the board in order to overcome this hurdle. Will you help create an executive summary of your presentation for our board?"

Kurt smiles as he shows Mary the ten-slide executive summary version of the value verification presentation he had stored in his backup slides. The sample Kent had sent Kurt included the executive summary, and Kurt had prepared the summary in case Mary's time was limited, but also to address the unknown. Kurt presented the full version he had prepared because Mary was detail oriented. But, he was ready in case she needed to cut to the chase. Now his executive summary would be presented to the board of directors of Costline Food Group. Kurt was well on his way to getting a major piece of business from Costline!

Congratulations! You just made your final presentation to Power, just like Kurt! Well, we hope you have, or will soon. When you work your way through this process the first time, parts of it may be a little tough or may make you uncomfortable. That's to be expected. The Zebra way is likely very different from your current sales approach. But when you present to Power, and you know Power is ready to help you get your project approved, the feeling is immeasurable—mostly because you will know in that moment that you've found the key to continued sales success! From here, you're moving into the final phase of the process, and if you've followed the Zebra way so far, you've done what's necessary to make it a breeze.

CATCH YOUR ZEBRA

CHAPTER 8

CONTRACT AND FORCE SUCCESS

MANY SALESPEOPLE DREAD CONTRACT negotiations. They know that even though it seems like the deal is done, it could still fall apart at any minute because of some surprise detail or a fight over cost. Enter the power of the Zebra.

In the Zebra Buying Cycle, contract negotiations come after you have already presented and verified your solution's value, provided financials that show how a decision to buy your product compares with all other uses of available capital, explained the key Power pain points your solution can address, and presented the solution cost that includes every element necessary to make the value possible. Having accomplished all of these steps ahead of time, you are immediately prepared to leverage them during the contract negotiations; you are in a powerful position to get the business, hold your price firm, and complete a win-win contract in a timely manner.

We start the Zebra Buying Cycle with an understanding of the Zebra and why it is important. After that, all of our business-development efforts target Zebras. But the real value for us and our customers happens when we achieve the endgame—Force Success. When we Force Success, we ensure the fulfillment of the promises and commitments Power will make to secure approval of the project or purchase.

Kurt has presented to the board at Costline Food Group, and Mary secured approval to move forward with the project subject to successful contract negotiations. Purchasing is unaware of the process C3 has conducted with Costline, so Kurt walks the purchasing executive through the process. He explains how the proposal was built to achieve all of the associated confirmed value. Mary Resch herself attended the first meeting. Kurt had also scheduled the first Force Success meeting with Mary, ninety days into the future, further justifying Mary's confidence that she was making an intelligent business decision.

Since he'd scheduled the meeting, Mary already knew exactly when Kurt was coming back. He had also reviewed the format of the Force Success meeting.

"Mary, when we meet in ninety days, we will review our project metrics. Additionally, the C3 project team will discuss what it has done right, what could be improved, and how it plans to improve in the future. We will help your project team members do

the same. This meeting, when conducted correctly, is collaborative and without finger-pointing. Sometimes the first meeting is a
little tense if all project members are not used to the format. Will
you help me present this process to your team so we can achieve
the desired collaborative results?"

"I like the C3 style," Mary says, smiling. "Of course I will."

Kurt and Mary have quickly become business friends.

Contract terms and conditions went through the normal itera-
tions, but the business case, agreed-upon pricing, and overall
business portion of the negotiations were more efficient—and
the overall process was faster—than anything Kurt had previously
experienced. And because Mary had a desire to start actually
achieving the $650,693 savings per month, she had personally
shepherded the project through legal. Contract negotiations that
often took weeks began and concluded all in the same week.

Kurt and the C3 sales and solution consulting team have conducted a Zebra Buying Cycle and closed a large C3 project in
just thirty-one days!

FOLLOW THROUGH TO FORCE SUCCESS

A sales representative's job doesn't end when a deal is closed. The
job ends—that is, the endgame is reached—when the customer
achieves the original project goals set during the sales process, the
goals established during the value verification. If you approach
every sales call and every strategic discussion with this focus in
mind, the positive, committed energy will be evident to your prospects, and you'll be able to leverage that commitment to their success for greater and greater results.

When we focus on forcing success, we begin with the end in mind. This focus changes each of the preceding sales cycle steps. As an organization, we are not finished until a customer successfully addresses Power's pain points and achieves the associated value. Therefore, we must

- Know from the outset what the pain points are.
- Ensure that our proposal is aligned to resolve them.
- Stand by our proposal during contract negotiations.
- Ensure that our delivery system constantly measures and reports our progress to Power.
- Know that we are not done until we help Power achieve the promises that led to the authorization of the project.

If you don't Force Success for your existing customers, the chances for winning over new prospects become increasingly bleak. Future success requires real past results, and real results are highly dependent upon forcing success.

Do you see the circle here? Force your customers to succeed, and you'll succeed right along with them. Allow your customers to fail, and well . . . you get it.

Without question, there is a niche in every market for a company that ensures delivery on project promises. Sell the way you would want to buy and you'll be on the Force Success path. This is the driver for the Force Success approach—an approach that is paramount to the success of contract negotiations.

NEGOTIATING THE CONTRACT

Contract negotiations don't build character, they reveal true character. And contract negotiations take on a completely different air when you follow the Zebra Buying Cycle—an air of partnership and commitment to mutual success. Your project is being sponsored by an executive who has specific pain points. The value of solving those pain points has been presented with impressive financial metrics. Power owns the sponsorship of the project and will shepherd it to conclusion. The monthly cost of indecision creates urgency to move forward now. All of these elements ease the negotiation process immensely.

Contract negotiation doesn't build character, it reveals true character.

During difficult contract negotiations, you'll specifically leverage the economic value added number that the value model produced. The EVA is particularly powerful at this time because of what it represents. EVA, like all of our financial metrics, removes all of the project costs from the benefit claim, but additionally includes the cost of capital. And the model you used goes one step further. Your EVA calculation, using the template model we provided, uses a 10 percent cost of capital or the prospect's operating margin, whichever is higher. Or, if the prospect has a particular project in mind with an even higher ROI, you can enter that percent in your value model, and the EVA will show how an investment in your solution compares with the competing project.

By using the highest of 10 percent, the prospect's operating margin, or even a high-yield competing project, your EVA number tells the prospect's financial decision makers the amount of value your project will produce over and above the financial results that could be expected if the prospect invested these same dollars in any other way!

As a salesperson, have you ever lost an opportunity because a manufacturing decision maker told you she definitively knew the value of adding another piece of equipment to their manufacturing project, but she couldn't really quantify the value of your proposed project? With a strong EVA in your pocket, you have an immediate answer to this question. The EVA is the value your solution generates beyond what would be possible if a manufacturer added more manufacturing capacity, if a distributor added another warehouse, or if a services firm added more people to deliver its services.

All of these financial metrics will help you hold your price firm. Why? Because you can easily say that your price includes everything necessary to make those metrics possible. The only way to lower your price is to remove components, and as soon as you remove components, you jeopardize the entire project. At this point, Power will not want to remove components, particularly now that you've presented results that have been verified by the users of the new system. You'll have the financial justification you need to say no to a price reduction. This is where the Force Success philosophy strengthens your position. You know what's necessary to force the success of your solution, and you can't back down from that commitment—and Power shouldn't expect you to.

Kurt's negotiation with Nem's is not as streamlined as it was with Costline. There is too much water under the bridge. Kurt has learned from the past mistakes at Nem's, though, and has added additional costs for education and has slowed the project ramp-up to allow ample time for Nem's employees to adopt to the new system.

Kurt initially used the EVA calculation automatically produced by the C3 Value Waterfall model. The EVA for Nem's when the

Direct & Indirect Savings	
ROI of this project over 3 years is:	829%
NPV of this project over 3 years is:	$13,953,620
EVA of this project over 3 years is:	$11,126,438
IRR of this project over 3 years is:	265%
Payback Period of this project is:	9 Months
Monthly cost of indecision is:	$497,643

Revised Financials with a Higher Cost of Capital

cost of capital was 10 percent was $11.5 million. But Mark Nem had told Kurt that there were other projects he was considering. One of those projects was a new warehouse with an expected rate of return of 24 percent. So Kurt changes the EVA cost of capital to 24 percent, a much more conservative number.

Kurt confidently presents the results to Mark Nem and his vice president of financing: "My solution will provide $11.1 million more value over three years than Nem's could hope to generate by adding more distribution capacity."

The VP of purchasing immediately questions a project component Kurt knew he would have to defend: service. "Listen, Kurt, I know we've had issues in the past, but our people are smarter now, and they've been through this process implementing a new supply-chain solution before. I just don't think we need the level of service you've included in your proposal. If you cut the level, it would reduce the cost of the project to a point that would make it easier to get final approval from the board."

Kurt feels himself wavering, wanting to rely on his old sales tactics and hack away at his proposal to get the contract signed. But he knows if he does that, he'll undercut everything he has worked for so far.

"I'm glad you raised this concern," he responds. "Let's return to our Value Waterfall—the source of our confirmed value. When I first met with you, Mark, I explained that other C3 customers of similar size and in the same industry had been able to drive larger amounts of unplanned incremental value. They have done this by following our recommendations for solution components *and* level of ongoing service. At this point, I have to have courage in my convictions because the facts are irrefutable: Our other customers have done it. Your people have verified it. We have assessed your people and the task at hand and have determined what is required to Force Success. This is the level of service required to achieve the promises Mark will make to gain approval for the CAR."

The VP considers Kurt's response for a moment. "It all comes back to the fact that you've done this before, doesn't it?"

"Yes, it really does. And if I let you go into the project ill-prepared to achieve the same level of success that our other customers have achieved, I haven't done my job."

Seeing Mark Nem nod his head in approval, the vice president of purchasing says, "Okay, let's move on . . ."

THE FORCE SUCCESS IMPLEMENTATION PLAN

So the contract has been signed, but your job isn't done yet, is it? It's not done until your client has achieved the value you've told them is possible. You made a deal: pay us this amount of money and this is what you'll achieve. If you don't hold up your end of the bargain, your credibility in the market will suffer—and so will your sales.

Forcing success means that the implementation plan you designed will enable your client to repeat the level of success that others have achieved with your solution. Force Success is configured to address Power's pain points. And Power's sponsorship and the process owners' buy-in from the value verification will fuel the implementation and help to eliminate some of the typical problems that crop up. But, when problems do surface, you will be in a powerful position to address them.

 WAKE-UP CALL

Complex sales usually involve complex implementations. Complex implementations require planning for the use of proper levels of resources, both internal and external to the prospect. That said, most complex sales cycles end in nondecision because Power doesn't believe her own people can achieve the results you advertise. Will they be able to adopt the change necessary to realize the potential of the project? Therefore, your proposal has to include the necessary education, consulting, support, and even the overall partner management needed to convince the people in Power that their people can achieve the expected results. Power has to know that you know you aren't done until you've helped them meet the promises they have to make to get the project approved.

Force Success Meetings

Like Kurt, as you negotiate the contract, you should schedule your first Force Success follow-up meeting, ideally within ninety days from the start of implementation. This lets Power know that you're definitely coming back and that you're committed! This meeting, and all subsequent Force Success meetings, should involve Power and any members of management that were involved in the value verification. In the first ninety days of any implementation, problems start to surface. So, during each Force Success meeting, you will assess the honest progress your team has made. You have to own any errors or shortcomings your company is responsible for, and to come to the meeting prepared to admit them and present solutions to fix these problems. And you should expect the same of the customer. It is your responsibility to make sure the customer owns the internal issues that could jeopardize success.

 WAKE-UP CALL

The first Force Success meeting often starts out a little tense because, honestly, the customer expects you to renege on your end of the deal. They don't think you'll take responsibility for issues that your company can and should solve. Once the customer's team sees that you are going to "set the example" and fix your issues, they will generally step up and do the same.

The second Force Success meeting usually feels entirely different from the first. Your proactive stance about solving problems in the first meeting will create a communication protocol that drives subsequent meetings. No one will want to come to the meetings unprepared. Both your team and the customer's team will communicate regularly. Few problems will go unsolved. The meetings will be more about reporting progress and less about blame for problems. When this shift happens, your project is on course to success.

The Force Success Approach to Service

Depending on what you sell and your position in the market, Force Success might require you to rethink how you deliver support. But in all cases, the customer pays for that support and service. Sometimes it's necessary to boost your support resources in order to adopt and deliver on a Force Success approach. Most companies install and leave. At best, something called a taillight guarantee is given: as your car's taillights disappear over the hill, so does the guarantee.

With a Force Success approach, you won't leave until Power agrees the metrics and promises have been achieved. But because you've sold your solution properly, you'll be getting paid for all the products and services you deliver. We aren't suggesting you add services where they are not needed. However, almost all implementations require change. Change requires change management. And complex implementations often require partnering with others to provide a complete solution. Management of that partnership and the partner solution is usually required. Make it your business to ensure that everything is managed well. You're not done until Power says the promises are met (Do we sound like a broken record? Good!), so make sure you scope the project properly and include all associated costs. Power won't hesitate to pay if you actually deliver.

How do you determine the level of service necessary to achieve the stated goals?

Every project manager has worked with a customer that was willing to drive the implementation to gain as much strategic and operational value as possible. Who are your most successful customers? What made them successful? What components of their success could be put into a repeatable model? All good implementation project managers can assess when and where a prospect (eventually a customer) will struggle. It's their job to provide extra help for that customer. If you involved that project manager in the Zebra Buying Cycle (specifically in the value verification, as recommended), you've sold their recommended levels of support, education, consulting, project management, implementation management, technical management, change management, partner management, and ongoing follow-up support required to achieve the agreed-upon results.

Kurt is reflecting on the different place he is in from where he was ninety days ago. Several high-profile Zebra opportunities have been closed successfully. The Nem's account, Costline Food Group, and other at-risk but strong Zebra opportunities have proven that the process works. Nem's hasn't completely forgiven past transgressions, but the company agreed to give C3 a small piece of the overall contract opportunity.

Kurt recalls his conversation with Mark Nem when Mark shared that the Nem's project manager didn't completely trust C3. C3 had burned them, and she wasn't about to buy in completely without making C3 prove it could deliver. She wanted to confirm that C3 was manifesting a real and permanent change. If it were up to her alone, C3 would have lost the business. Mark, however, had decided to give C3 another chance, but he warned

Kurt that the Force Success concept sold so enthusiastically is viewed with caution at Nem's and must be proven before Kurt's division can win the rest of the contract.

After ending his conversation with Mark, Kurt realized that had he continued to chase all of the non-Zebras in the pipeline, he never would have had the resources to focus on Nem's or the other at-risk Zebras. With the new Zebra focus, Kurt is able to put additional resources and added focus on all of the opportunities worthy of C3's best but limited sales resources. Now that the ninety days has expired, Kurt and the board can see definite positive progress.

We've given you everything you need to sell to your Zebra, close the sale, and ensure that your new customer is a happy one. You know what you need to make your product successful; we've just shown you how to sell it that way. The last bit of advice we can offer is how to force the success of our product—the Zebra Buying Cycle—in your organization.

CHAPTER 9

OPERATIONS FOR THE ZEBRA WAY

YOU MAY HAVE NOTICED THAT NOWHERE IN this book does it say that you have to have the *best* product or service or solution to succeed. Rather, you have to have a *viable* solution with a compelling strategy, and the Zebra approach can help you create a compelling strategy! Besides, no competitive advantage is forever. Competition will always catch up. If you sell your strengths, address your weaknesses, and Force Success, you'll win more business, regardless of your competitive environment. It's as simple as that!

The principle of the Zebra is not difficult, but the execution might not be so easy. It will involve hard decisions and self-discipline, and your resolve will be tested. You will find out just how well you understand Zebra principles and discover the strength of your resolve as you try to put your newfound methodology into practice. To help you through this tough time, we're going to give you some more tools and ideas that will enable you to force the success of the Zebra way in your organization.

The Zebra philosophy makes sense intuitively, but it must be converted into a repeatable process and melded with everyday business in sales, pre- and post-sales support, and customer service. No single piece of this process can be truly effective on its own, and much like the sale of a solution, a process is only as good as its implementation. No amount of effort can make up for failing to implement the right sales practices. For that reason, you have to change the way you think about sales as a whole.

Forcing the success of the Zebra way within your own organization will take some time. Not only do you have to change your thinking, you have to change the thinking of your salespeople and all of the people involved in selling and supporting your products in the market. The first critical change in perspective is understanding that sales (or business, for that matter) is not a democracy, and that can be a hard pill to swallow.

SALES IS NOT A DEMOCRACY

Greater success in sales is all about applying your limited resources more intelligently, and this is one of the primary benefits of the Zebra way. The way things are today, you probably get a lot of requests for demonstrations, simulations, studies, and so on. Any one of these activities can easily consume a week. Most often, resources are assigned to activities on a first-come-first-served basis—but should they be?

At this point, we hope your answer is "Of course not." A manager's greatest responsibility is *to make the best use of limited resources* and, in essence, *decide what not to do.* No one's energy may be wasted. Resources shouldn't be assigned equally for every potential prospect on the basis of first come, first served. It doesn't make sense to deploy resources as they are requested just because they are requested. A salesperson's greatest responsibility should be to know when he can win a deal and request that resources be spent on those deals that present the best opportunities for the company.

Politics are definitely involved in any decision, but a sales staff is not a democracy. Salespeople are not all created equal. In fact, more than 80 percent of sales come from the top 20 percent of sales representatives. The same trend holds with presales consultants. Top-performing salespeople are already rewarded through compensation based on how much they sell. The more they sell, the higher the commission rate and the more pay and bonuses they receive. Reward resources are allocated to those who are most deserving, and so should your sales resources.

 WAKE-UP CALL

If you absolutely trust your best salespeople when they tell you they've got a Zebra in their sights, then you can feel confident in giving them the resources they need to make the deal happen. But you need to score them, measure their success, and know their individual pipeline close rates. There's an old saying in management: You can't expect what you don't inspect. Inspect your salespeople's pipelines and root out the non-Zebras.

Valuable sales resources should be focused on the best Zebra opportunities, and they should be allocated the same way. Focusing sales resources on those opportunities that best fit the Zebra also demands fewer of those resources and ties them up for a shorter period of time, thus maximizing the potential of existing limited resources. The opportunity cost of any sales endeavor requires using your best people and most valuable resources where you have the best opportunity to win. The Zebra approach also helps to avoid the negative costs associated with poor sales execution. When resources are properly aligned with opportunities, costs are properly aligned with revenues, maximizing the potential for generating profit.

Fortunately, salespeople are used to frequent change and facing adversity. If there is one area of any organization most able to embrace change, it's the sales department. In fact, most successful salespeople achieve results despite the organizational roadblocks put in their path. The Zebra philosophy provides you with a way to eliminate the roadblocks. When others try to force time-wasting requests upon you, you can resist them, even though it may feel unnatural to you at first. The Zebra will naturally become the pinnacle philosophy that drives how you spend your time and your resources.

LOOK AT YOUR SALES TEAM HONESTLY

Sales change created by using the Zebra methodology should cause a company to reassess the type of talent needed to sell its products. The Zebra and Zebra Buying Cycle address where you're most successful. It's natural and smart to assess your current and future hires against your new model. In doing so, you'll find that not all of them will make the cut. You may not use a performance rating system within your company, but we've used the following categories to help companies assess their salespeople in Zebra terms:

1. This salesperson shouldn't be allowed anywhere near a prospect or a customer.
2. This salesperson is almost as bad as a 1 but looks good enough as long as he doesn't open his mouth.

3. This salesperson has personal presence but no real sales sense. She thinks the product sells itself and that all salespeople, like herself, just take orders. This individual is a sales manager's worst nightmare because executive managers in many companies already think the product sells itself. When this attitude penetrates sales, the results are always bad.

4. This person is like a bad car salesperson. He talks but doesn't listen. He thinks the world revolves around him, and he doesn't know what he doesn't know. A category 4 salesperson is a hard charger who uses a full-frontal sales approach in every sales situation. He is usually combative toward prospects as well as fellow employees.

Anyone who rates 4 or below should be reassigned or let go as soon as possible. If you can't in good conscience move this problem person to another area of the organization, own your mistake and let him go!

5. This salesperson has potential if she knows what she doesn't know. She is constantly asking questions and absorbing everything. She has great potential if she asks *good* questions and greater potential if she asks questions even you have difficulty answering. She is beginning to understand where she *should* win, but she can't yet tell where she is *going* to win. Apathy or nondecision is this person's biggest sales challenge. Young 5s have been known to say, "I didn't lose: they didn't buy from *anyone*," or, "They liked *me* but just didn't want to buy from my *company*." She doesn't yet understand what is wrong with these reactions. This person should be mentored. If her progress plateaus, she should be put on a probationary plan that includes measurable objectives.

6. This salesperson shows real promise. He has sales instincts and listens to them. He understands that sales' number-one job is to determine where we are going to win. He shows respect for and values our people resources. He listens to and shows empathy toward a prospect's needs. He understands that the language for selling to Power is different from the language used for other audiences, and he has demonstrated a willingness to learn the language of Power. This person should be mentored. If his progress plateaus, he should be put on a probationary plan that has measurable objectives.

7. This salesperson understands the sales world. She consistently achieves her sales quota. Although she's not a superstar, she is a valued performer. A 7 is able to work well with management and operations-level personnel and knows how to turn sales cycles into Zebra Buying Cycles. She handles challenging buying cycle steps with grace and diplomacy to ensure that each step serves both her company and the prospect. A 7 who covers her costs but has no upward potential should be allowed to quietly continue where she is. A 7 with potential should be nurtured, mentored, and groomed for greater responsibilities.

8. This salesperson consistently knows when he has a Zebra. He knows not only where he *should* win but also where and when he *will* win. He has the innate "street smarts" necessary to drive Zebra Buying Cycles with Power-level sponsorship to successful conclusion. He values his family, self, customer, and company.

9. This salesperson has the business acumen to establish sales relationships in Zebra accounts at user, operational/managerial, and Power levels. She trusts her instincts, no matter how illogical her impression might seem; she knows that sooner or later the truth behind the feeling will reveal

itself. A 9 drives consistent, profitable, and clean revenue. She knows the value of forcing success and how to Force Success within client companies. She consistently closes 80 percent of her pipeline.

10. This salesperson is the ideal. He has the conviction and business knowledge to assess prospect-requested sales-cycle steps, accepting and executing those that are good for both the prospect and his own company, and tactfully rejecting or changing steps that serve neither party. A 10 is valued by the prospect company and invited into the circle of Power as a trusted friend. A 10 will have made quota nine out of ten years, if not ten out of ten. He closes 90 percent of the accounts that hit his sales pipeline because he knows how to target, identify, and bring home Zebras.

Measuring True Sales Productivity

In the business world, we learn to play a lot of games with numbers. Numeric measurements can be twisted, manipulated, and presented in many different ways to support any number of desired conclusions for a given scenario. For example, you could keep head count artificially low by not hiring when necessary and by planning ahead for the next year, thus raising the productivity-per-sales head count without actually doing what is right for the business. Sales management and salespeople could also sandbag or be very frugal about forecasting and thereby increase their pipeline close rate. They could delay the recording of deals, improving the average age of their pipeline. Again, both of these measurements, if abused, would indicate a positive direction for the business and foster less-than-positive behavior.

But no one could play games with the numbers if success were measured only by overall improvement. *That* is how you should measure sales success: by considering the metrics listed below—*all at once*. Think of it! We'd undoubtedly grow our business if we moved all the measurements in the right direction simultaneously.

Therefore, sales productivity should be measured in terms of

- actual sales results as percentage of quota by division, sales manager, sales representative, and presales consultant
- revenue generated per sales team member
- revenue generated per sales expense dollar
- pipeline close rate
- average age of pipeline (because time kills all deals), by salesperson, by sales manager, by divisional vice president of sales
- average Zebra score at the beginning of the quarter required to predict quarter-end revenue with 90 percent accuracy

FORECASTING

We're betting that your present forecasting process most likely doesn't provide you with a consistent, repeatable way to predict revenue. Specifically, you probably don't have a reliable way to evaluate the status of each of the accounts in your pipeline. How can you improve your pipeline close-rate percentage if you have a broken forecasting process? The simple fact is that an account in your pipeline at the demo stage of a sales cycle won't necessarily ever lead to revenue, yet it's a common practice to treat all accounts at that stage the same way in terms of forecasting. There has to be a better way of understanding the potential that actually exists in your pipeline.

So that you don't have to blindly approach this new and somewhat foreign Zebra philosophy through trial and error, it's imperative to set new benchmarks that will assure your progress. Start by setting some short-term goals. Get a handle on your current average sales cycle length and current level of product discounting so you can set proper metrics. Specifically, the first benchmarks should measure your progress ninety days A.Z. (After Zebra).

 WAKE-UP CALL

What should you expect ninety days A.Z.?

- Overall pipeline will go down before it goes up.
- Pipeline close rate will improve from present 15 percent to 25 percent in first ninety days.
- Buying cycles will be shorter.
- You will achieve product differentiation.
- You will reduce discounting.

Setting short-term goals is very important, but if you fail to plan for the long run, you might as well have planned to fail! The Zebra Buying Cycle Pipeline Forecast (see page 224) is one possible way to address this issue. To formulate a successful plan for forecasting your pipeline, begin with the desired end in mind and work back from there. To do that, you have to be sure you really understand the Power-level pain points of your customers and prospects. This is where most salespeople fall short, because you can't just focus on operational-level business issues and assume that they will drive revenue.

The Zebra Buying Cycle Pipeline Forecast ties directly into the Zebra steps. Notice that the first two steps are prospecting

Zebra Buying Cycle Pipeline Forecast

	Prospecting	Upside				Commit		
	-1 Identify Zebras	0 Confirm PBIs Close with Hypothesis of Value	1 Meet with Power	2 Conduct Value Verification	3 Copresent Value Verification Findings	4 Negotiate Contract	5 Close Deal	6 Force Success
Objective of Sales Stage	• Use Zebra profile to research territory and generate leads • Develop business issues by industries	• Contact prospect	• Get Power to confirm business issues and urgency	• Conduct on-site discovery to verify hypothesis of value	• Present verified value back to POWER	• C3 selected • CAR process begins	• Negotiate, agree on pricing and terms, and formalize commitment	• Ensure fulfillment of promises that Power made to get project approved
Major Sales Activities & Use of Tools	• Target firms or business units by using the Push-button Zebra • Define PBIs • Identify key executives • Secure appointments	• Research account to discover C3 tie-ins to PBI • Identify similar customers • Confirm urgency to address business issues • Confirm Push-button Zebra score of at least 16 • Secure Power level appt. • Prepare value hypothesis	• Meet with Power; executive presentation • Confirm business issues, compelling need and power sponsorship • Understand procurement (CAR) process • Confirm Push-button Zebra score of at least 23	• Complete Power-sponsored Value Verification (coauthor presentation with process owners) • Identify current situation and best practices, and quantify improvements • Develop Force Success proposal with help of C3 services group • Confirm Push-button Zebra score of at least 27	• Make coauthored Value Verification presentation to Power • Simulate solution with screen shots • Present Force Success proposal • Provide proof you have done this before (references) • Begin discussing business terms of the deal • Identify any gaps in solution	• Gaps resolved • Operations, management, and IT recommend C3 • Power verbally agrees to do business • CAR presented and approved • Contracts sent	• Agree on pricing • Resolve legal and business issues • Ensure that no known factors will prohibit booking business in the month named • Sign contract and collect down payment	• Conduct turnover account from sales to postsale services • Set date for first Force Success meeting between C3 management (sales and services) and client executive management

steps, and the associated values are -1 and 0. This is very much by design. We don't forecast revenue from accounts at steps -1 or 0 in our pipeline totals. Notice also that before something is even considered to be on the forecast at step 1 and beyond, Power has to confirm business issues and urgency.

There are additional "gating points" for all of the steps in the forecast. For instance, before you move a prospect beyond step 1, you must also understand the CAR process used to get projects like yours approved. You can also use your Push-button Zebra to establish gating points by determining a verifiable Z-score threshold for moving beyond each stage and using more resources. This will help you be disciplined and methodical in your forecasting approach, and it's an excellent cross-reference to avoid reverting back to the less-disciplined approach of simply launching your valuable limited resources at a prospect with blind hope. Sales and sales management must work as a team to confirm that all the gating points have been addressed before a prospect can move up the chart to the next step in the forecasting process.

Do you see how nicely all of the steps tie in to our Zebra steps? And do you also see how this process is self-policing?

Notice how once you get through step 2, you will have verified the value of your product and created a Force Success proposal designed to accomplish all of Power's pain points. By the end of step 3, you will have presented the value verification results to Power, and the prospect is ready to be counted as a commit account for the quarter.

Using the Zebra Buying Cycle Pipeline Forecast, your accounts in steps 1 through 6 will attain a high level of predictability, and your forecast numbers will become much more dependable than they have been in the past. This process also improves communication between sales managers and salespeople because it provides standardization that improves consistency from one individual to another.

Combining the Zebra Buying Cycle Pipeline Forecast with a given Zebra score from the Push-button Zebra provides you with a way to be confident in the amount of business you will bring in for a quarter. The mystical guesswork historically involved with forecasting is effectively eliminated.

These tools provide discipline through process when practicing the Zebra philosophy, and that is the heart of why it is possible to achieve pipeline close rates of more than 80 percent in less than one year. Given that fact, it is a reasonable ninety-day goal to improve your current pipeline close rate by 10 percent. It also seems reasonable that if you focus only on areas where your solution brings unique competitive advantage (and therefore product differentiation) to your customers and combine this with a true focus on Power, you'll have increased your *real* opportunities and you can expect shorter buying cycles. It's only logical to conclude that if you bring more value, you can expect higher overall profit margins because you won't have to resort to discounting to close business, and your Force Success proposals will naturally be more robust.

WHAT ABOUT COMPETITION?

How do you adjust your Zebra strategy based on competition? You most likely face some very worthy competitors, and some of them may even have a Zebra similar to yours. Competition plays an important role in the Zebra process; it helps identify the weaknesses in your solution. Every solution for every prospect has gaps. If your gaps are strategically critical to a particular solution, you have to address them. If you don't address them, your competition will, and they will win more than their share of deals.

WAKE-UP CALL

It's a good idea to include an analysis of your competitors in your Zebra profile. How might your competitors pursue and meet the needs of your Zebras? Good competition means your prospect has found the companies that offer the best options to address Power's pain points; in this situation, someone will get a piece of business. If the best competitors in your field are not in on a deal, you might want to ask yourself whether the opportunity is even real and whether you should be spending resources pursuing it.

The best way to address your gaps is to be honest about them with the prospect and to share how you plan to address them. This process inoculates the prospect from aggressive negative selling by your competition. You might find that once you communicate a gap, your prospect will even strategize with you about how to address it. These prospects often will not even listen to a competitor who tries to sell by pointing out the gaps you have already discussed.

Kurt walks into a meeting with his management team to discuss their progress in the past ninety days. He greets everybody and then dives in, excited to talk about what they've accomplished and where to keep pushing.

The team discusses how sales management and presales have started to challenge the sales organization to evaluate prospects against the Zebra, forcing sales to identify strengths and strategize gaps before scheduled appointments. The new sales forecasting process has provided some tough but necessary discussions before key resources are deployed to accounts. The result: Kurt's "Zebrafied" pipeline is now much cleaner and better reflects closable business. A forecast from any one region is now substantially similar to the forecasts from all the other regions.

"A key part of this process is to be first—first because we win, first to change the playing field, or first to exit the deal," Kurt tells his team. "The decisions of whether to engage and how to engage are a big part of this process. Each cross-functional team member brings a unique perspective and expertise to the discussion to establish where we *should* win. The role of the sales representative should be to communicate where we are *going to win*. And this will help us keep pulling away from the drive for meaningless activity."

"Well, activity certainly doesn't put any money in my wallet," says sales manager Jennifer.

"It puts money in mine," grouses Lou. "Right now, my team gets paid for generating leads."

"Lou, you have a point," Kurt says. "We should look at your group's compensation plan; we should tie business development to actual sales results instead of to activity. That way, we'll all be pulling in the same direction."

"But Kurt, what happens when we decide to answer an RFP?" Dave asks. "What happens when we meet with a prospect, are very involved in a sales cycle, have gone through expensive steps like demonstrations and simulations, and we learn things that cause us to question whether we have a Zebra?"

"I asked that question of Kent last week," Kurt says, "and he explained that all of these expensive steps are sunk costs. A Zebra discussion should take place before resources are deployed for each advancing step of a cycle. If we learn that an account is not a Zebra at the end of a cycle step, or even at the end of a long, expensive, and nearly complete buying cycle, we reevaluate and make a new decision."

"That's easier to say than it is to do," Jennifer says with concern.

"Yeah, the Zebra isn't always black and white—pun intended," Lou says, to groans from the rest of the team.

"No question," Kurt says. "That's why Kent and his team say that this process is part science and part art. They call this the 'science of deliberate selling and the art of sales execution.' Using the process is a science, and science requires discipline. The cross-functional aspect of this process helps keep all team members honest with themselves."

Dick, manager of contract negotiations, points out a matter of hierarchy. "Who ultimately decides whether we continue to pursue a prospect, walk away, or try to change the playing field of a deal?"

"The person who owns the quota has to have the power to decide," Jennifer interjects before Kurt can respond. "I have also talked with Kent's sales representatives. I've learned that the cross-functional team provides strong input, just as Kurt has been pointing out, but at the end of the day, the responsible person is the one who owns the quota and will lose his or her job if quota is not met. The sales representative, and ideally his or her sales manager, makes the final decision on each sales opportunity."

At this point, all eyes return to Kurt.

"Jennifer is on target here," he confirms. "Why do you think we pay our best salespeople as much as many CEOs in smaller companies earn? They're the artists who own responsibility for the 'art' aspect of this process. We can strategize all we want about how to find and get to Power in our target accounts, but as you all know, there are no executives in any company we've ever pursued who use the word *Power* in their title. Figuring out who Power is, earning the right to meet at that level, and possessing the business acumen necessary to stay at that level are what comprise the art of sales execution."

Kurt and his team continue to talk about their Zebra processes long into the afternoon.

BEFORE IT CAN GO UP, IT MUST COME DOWN

When you begin following the Zebra methodology, you are going to inevitably eliminate some deals in your current sales pipeline that aren't Zebras. That means that the overall number of opportunities and dollars in your pipeline will initially go down. And even though salespeople become more productive right away, they don't look good on paper if you're measuring activity levels. They aren't pursuing accounts that don't make it through the Zebra filter. So, as you begin to use the Zebra methodology, your sales pipeline will shrink, and it may appear as though you're going backward. This is an illusion. But because of this impression, initial implementation of the Zebra philosophy may result in at least some degree of struggle against conventional company sales thinking.

PRACTICE MAKES PERFECT

There's only one reason why the methods presented here won't work, and that's if there isn't any demand for your solutions. If that's the case—and 99 percent of the time it isn't—then, and only then, should you give up. More likely your costs of selling are up, discounting is high, and margins are down. You must be determined to proactively affect change. As you progress through what has been discussed thus far, you're going to run into a few additional bottlenecks. One of these bottlenecks will occur as you try to use your existing business development resources to find a way to get to Power within your existing customer base. If your business development team hasn't been able to uncover Power within your customer base or prospect base in the past, much less set appointments with Power, what makes you think they can now?

Fortunately, this scenario is pretty common, and you're not alone. It's probably a safe bet that very few of your sales coworkers—and few salespeople among your competitors, for that matter—have relationships with Power. Nor do many know who Power is within their customer accounts. This is an age-old problem in sales, so don't feel bad that you haven't solved it, and don't expect to completely solve it the first time you try using the Zebra approach. Do expect to make progress toward a solution, though.

Don't act insane. For one thing, you'll scare away potential prospects, and (more seriously) you are practicing sales insanity when you do the same thing you did yesterday and expect a different result. You're going to need repeated practice calling on existing customers to find Power and test the Power-level pain points you address. Your initial goal should be getting appointments with Power within your base of customers. Once you get to Power and conduct audits with your existing customers, you'll have confirmed Power's pain points and gathered proof of the quantifiable value your solution can provide. You'll also have that proof, and quotable examples of it, in your customers' own words, not the usual marketing speak. These quotable examples from your customers are testimonials to your solution's effectiveness, and you should begin trying to work them into your approach. It's going to be tempting to revert back to old habits as you meet resistance in your quest to become a better salesperson, but you must avoid that temptation. As you practice learning these new skills, your reward will be an ability to identify and connect with Power, and things will only get easier and more natural for you the longer you keep at it.

You now can present to Power the results of your audits: your prediction of value and your assessment of whether your solution is being used to its maximum advantage. The win for your customer is a road map for how to achieve unrealized value within the solution they have already purchased. The win for you is the chance to meet Power in your customer base, learn what pain points drove the purchase of your solution, and uncover consulting and potential add-on business opportunities. Perhaps the most important benefit, however, is learning how to repeat these stories of value, with conviction, to Power in prospect companies in your pipeline.

Kurt has just returned from a monthly managers' meeting at headquarters for all division heads, where news of his team's past three months of success had already traveled. Kurt and his team are surpassing their own expectations from the Zebra process. Team members now close better than 50 percent of the deals in their pipeline, leading to an overall sales increase of 150 percent in the most recent month.

Bertha, the customer relationship management system, is now used religiously to monitor true sales progress, not activity levels.

C3 has closed a few multimillion-dollar transactions just in the last ninety days. The average length of buying cycles has been reduced by more than 25 percent.

Kurt and Kent were praised heavily at the meeting, not so much by Scotty, but by Scotty's boss, Ray Church. And that was a curious interaction.

Kurt sits down behind his desk just as the phone rings. It's Kent.

"Kurt," Kent begins, "Have you heard the news?"

"What's up?"

"Scotty resigned, and Ray has asked me to take over as president of C3!"

"Wow! When did this happen?"

"Just after the meeting," Kent answers. "It turns out that Ray sat down with Scotty directly after our meeting and told him the board had voted to remove him as president and CEO. Ray will now be CEO, and I will be president."

"This is *really* great news, Kent!" says Kurt, barely able to contain his enthusiasm. "When will we be making a formal announcement?"

"It just went out on the wire and over the Web. That was why I asked you if you'd heard the news."

"I haven't even opened my computer yet," Kurt explains. "What does the announcement say?"

"I'll read it to you," Kent offers. "William N. Scott has announced his resignation after twelve years of service to C3, a New York conglomerate. Scott says he has elected to spend more time with his family."

"Why do they always say that?" Kurt interrupts. "Spend more time with his family? Scotty doesn't have any kids, and his wife divorced him last year after thirty-two years of marriage. Family, my eye!"

Kent continues seriously, "'I'm spending more time with my family' is code for 'I got fired.' I don't mean to be insensitive to Scotty, but this will actually be better for him and for C3. Scotty was beginning to look very tired, and I don't think his health is very good."

Kent pauses. "Kurt, I have one more thing to discuss with you," he says in a hushed tone. "Before I accepted the responsibility as president of C3, I received a few verbal commitments from Ray in support of specific changes I knew we needed to make to continue turning C3 around. I'm going to need your help, buddy..."

When Kurt hangs up the phone, he feels flattered and excited. C3 is about to embark on another adventure—and he is the new COO!

Perhaps at this point you have already realized the benefit of your sales cycles beginning to shorten, and you may even have closed several Zebra opportunities successfully. That's the way all of this should go for you! With this new focus and discipline you *should* find great reward, and those rewards should come early and often. It is not unreasonable to expect that the first month you practice the Zebra may be the best sales month you've had in years. Don't confuse sales with the value of your overall pipeline, which may initially go down. Many companies and individuals have seen immediate success because they stopped working on the 85 percent waste in their old pipeline forecast. Mind-set is critical, and this would be a very positive mind-set to use when approaching your daily routine.

Six months into the Year of the Zebra—your first year using this new process—we believe you will be able to predict the amount of revenue you will book by the time the next quarter of business closes. We are so confident in this process that we can personally promise you that if you stick closely to following the principles in this book, you will close at least 60 percent of your forecast business that has a Zebra score above your threshold level (usually a Z-score at or about 23). Some of you may even realize in excess of 80 percent accuracy with your forecasts. You will be able to directly predict where you will *win*. Now, ladies and gentlemen, have you ever heard of a more meaningful sales metric?

Every deal in your pipeline is now discussed in terms of your company-to-company strengths and weaknesses, operational fit and concerns, technology fit and concerns, services fit and concerns, funding, and ROI. The process gets you in front of Power and allows you to accurately determine your strengths and weaknesses relative to every prospect in your forecast. You are now able to quantify your findings in a universal language that anyone can understand. You can quickly determine where you are strong and where your challenges exist, and you can put the proper energy and resources into the promising opportunities so you can accentuate your strengths and address your weaknesses. You are now more prepared for the ever-accelerating speed of today's sales world. Do you see the power in this?

Add to this the fact that you can now confidently look a customer or prospect in the eye and know that you have sold and negotiated a Force Success contract with enough education, consulting, professional services, and change management to all but guarantee that your customers will achieve the promises they make regarding the purchase of your solution. Your reference-worthy customers in your customer base should hit or be close to 100 percent, and you have one powerful prescription for success! Even if some of your customers are unhappy at a given moment, they now know and will probably be willing to reference the Force Success methodology. They will therefore be willing to share with others how the process will eventually help improve their current dissatisfaction.

The salespeople in your organization will feel empowered to challenge and significantly contribute to sales and sales strategy decisions. They will produce more results and therefore receive higher commissions while performing fewer demonstrations and traveling fewer days in the week.

So enjoy the next year . . . the Year of the Zebra!

THANKS

IF YOU WANT CREATIVITY AND INNOVATION that bends, but doesn't break, the classic book-publishing paradigm, you want Greenleaf Book Group. If you want an end product that is better than what you can get from the big guys and light years beyond what you can do yourself, you need Greenleaf.

We sound like a commercial for Greenleaf Book Group because our experience has been excellent. Lari Bishop all but coauthored this book. Her business acumen, writing, and organizational abilities kept the integrity of the original version of our book—which, by the way, we were very proud of—and turned it into the polished market ready product you now hold in your hands. Thanks to Sheila Parr, the book cover stands out and catches your eye—does it not? Well, that is Greenleaf expertise at work. The bookstores and wholesalers respect Meg La Borde, Ryan Wheeler, Kristen Sears, and Clint Greenleaf. They have a strong reputation, and we get to ride it. We like that!

Finally we wanted to thank our friends who read the first versions of *Selling to Zebras* and liked it enough to encourage us. You sustained us. I am embarrassed to say this project took years. Yes, years. Kevin, Jim, Patricia, Glenn, and others: thank you for your contributions. You have made Zebras a better read and an even more effective tool and process.

Thank you all for helping *Selling to Zebras* come to life!

INDEX